Contents

Chapters

1. Common Issues, Helpful Guidelines

2. Messages from God and Jesus

From God

From Jesus

3. Help from Other Writers

From Matt Kahn

From Joel Goldsmith

From Mary Barbara Jankowski

4. Freedom Worksheets

Acknowledgements

First and foremost, I have to acknowledge Jesus the Christ for being the way-shower for me to follow. His love is overwhelming and unending, and he is always there for me. He channeled "A Course in Miracles" and "The Way of Mastery" which turned my life around and made possible this guidebook.

Next would be Mary Barbara Jankowski,, author of "A Path to Peace", a complement to "A Course in Miracles", whose unending love and dedication to weekly A.C.I.M. groups have radically influenced me for the last 18 years. It was her prompting that made this book possible.

Then there are the many authors and speakers on my spiritual path. The first to come to mind is Wayne Dyer (God rest his soul). Add to that, Marianne Williamson, Gary Renard, Gregg Braden, Byron Katie, Matt Kahn, Abraham-Hicks, Eckart Tolle, Kim Michaels, Michele O'donnell, Joel Goldsmith, Alan Robothem, and many more.

This wouldn't be complete without mentioning the numerous people who unknowingly helped me by just being in my life, and being themselves. These would be the ones I have judged, resisted, directed anger to, or disapproved of in any way. They are the ones who so generously taught me how to be accepting, to love, and to serve all, no matter what they do or say, no matter of personality, race, religion, or any differences. I learned from some of them, that when I perceived an attack from another, it was really a call for love. When I forgave them and myself, I was free!

Introduction

I never intended to be a writer and certainly not an author. I was unwittingly guided by my higher self, what I call the Holy Spirit, to accomplish the REAL purpose I came into this world to fulfill.

"Divine Mastery" is a compilation of many short and practical spiritual/psychological essays designed to help you obtain mastery over your life.This no-nonsense, easy to read guide is short, but concise, and when applied, will bring you to an enlightened state of mind in the shortest period of time.

As this book becomes your daily practice, you will be guided to your own path of service, as was I. In the interim, it will open your mind and heart to unconditional love, where peace, love, joy, wisdom, abundance, power, and real freedom awaits you.

In Chapter 3, you will find worksheets that will enhance and accelerate your internalization of the material. I wholeheartedly encourage you to copy and use them. You will also find several channeled messages from Jesus, even God, along with a few short writings from well-respected spiritual teachers and authors.

I humbly present you with this book, my gift to you. My love goes out to each of you, knowing that you will glean exactly what you need from this work. This is a guide, a roadmap if you will, designed to rekindle your lost memory of the truth of who you are, while enlightening your mind and transforming your life.

1. Common Issues, Helpful Guidelines

Fear and Security
Based on "A Course in Miracles"

It seems many 'Course' students want to sidestep the facts that Jesus has laid out for us in "A Course in Miracles" He said the body is not real, just a temporary manifestation, and we are not bodies, we are free spirits. You can make an idol out of the body very easily, and all idols are of the ego (fear) and not of God (love). Here are some ways we make an idol of the body:

- Fearing loss of the body by death (see all fears below).

- Fearing disease (health insurance, vaccinations, drugs, fear of germs, etc., etc.)
- Fearing physical harm to the body (from accidents, perpetrators, etc.)
- Fearing pain of the body (drugs)
- Fearing aging of the body(makeup, creams, plastic surgery, facelifts, hair color, hair removal, drugs and supplements, invasive surgeries.
- Fearing the exploitation of the body (rape, etc.)

Of course body fears are just the tip of the iceberg. Many other fears are based on our past experiences, especially in childhood. Even other fears are related to loss. Fears control your life more than you might think. Take the time to list all your fears. Remember that it is not bad or wrong to have fears, but they do hinder your way to freedom. The only thing to fear is fear itself. List your fears as completely and honestly as you are able. Then ask that they be removed from your memory, so you no longer hurt yourself with them.

So now what about security? Is there truly any such thing as security in this world? An emphatic NO! No amount of fear, money, care, insurance, carefulness, alertness, door locks, guns and other protective devices, secure buildings and vehicles, armored guards, proper diets, hospitals, doctors, surgeons, or quality food, air, and water, can ever give you any kind of security in this world. As long as you continue to think so, you will be imprisoned by your mind and you will never be free! Enlightenment is totally contingent on this factor, so we must accept the absurdity of these fears and protective solutions, and expand our thinking now, if we are to achieve mastery over our lives, and experience REAL freedom.

Manipulation

Manipulation is so widely accepted and expected that we hardly know when we are doing it and when it is perpetrated unto us. It is usually used to control or influence others. Some are so proficient at it that most are unaware they are even being subjected to its ugly grip.

Of course, all manipulators are not equal. All sociopaths are unscrupulous, master manipulators. Their only objective is to get what they want, at anybody's expense. Money, power, and control are their objectives. They have no guilt and no conscience. They see people only as pawns, a means to an end, even if it means assassination. We see these people a lot in most governments, even in the United States. The Armed Forces has manipulated men to believe it is alright to murder other humans in the interest of national security, when in truth, wars were fought to fuel the economy and make the rich and powerful bankers even richer.

Then there are those who have hidden behind the cloak of religion. They have been known to use scare tactics to control you. They may say things like:

- God commanded you to give 10%.

- If you don't attend this church and believe what we do, you will burn in hell.
- That isn't a godly thing to say. Aren't you a Christian?
- The Bible says you should_____.

Sales people can be notorious manipulators who may say almost anything to obtain a sale, even outright lies. Examples:
- You will never see the price this low again
- Every household needs this.
- I can only guarantee this price today.
- Let me tell you why you really need this.
- Nobody can beat our quality and price.
- This looks so good on you!
- You will look years younger.
- This will make your home worth much more.
- I am giving you a special price just for today.
- Wear this and get lots more dates.

Other manipulators appear as just regular people, even highly respected people, who believe they are better than others and should get whatever they want when they want it. Many of these personalities were spoiled as children. Have you known anybody that rarely will take no for an answer? He will cleverly say things, usually questions, that are so convincing, that you may question your own good judgment, or even your sanity. Here are some typical ones:
- I can't believe you would say that to me.

- What did I say that would make you feel that way?
- You shouldn't be offended.
- I was only trying to help.
- What were you thinking?
- I don't deserve to be talked to that way.
- Would you just leave me alone!
- Don't you have any common sense?
- I don't have time to listen to that.
- We're not going to talk about this anymore.
- It's not my fault, it's yours.
- I don't have to listen to that.
- I would never purposely hurt you.
- Can't you do anything right?
- That's not a nice thing to say.

With this information, my hope is that you will catch yourself manipulating others and stop, and conversely, be aware of when another is attempting to manipulate you and not succumb to it. Let's stop this terrible form of dishonesty and disrespect in the world. What do you think?

I Can Give Up Defensiveness

For many of us, being defensive has always been a way of life and seemingly useful and important. After all, if I don't defend myself, who will? Well I'm here to tell you that you bought into a worldview "norm", a mass belief, that does NOT serve you or anyone else. Here is why:

- In the first place, we are all perfect, whole and complete, as God created us, therefore we do not need to prove our innocence to anyone or ourselves. How could you, or why would you, even attempt to defend perfection?
- Next, defending oneself causes arguments and separation, caused by projecting your own (false) guilt onto someone else by making him wrong. This is an unconscious way of avoiding the uncomfortable experience of feeling guilty.
- Thirdly, we lose our peace in this defensive process. In "A Course in Miracles" it states, Would you rather be right or happy? We must remember that in truth, anyone's perceived attack or judgement on us is only a call for love and needs only be returned WITH love.

So instead of impulsively reacting in defense, stop and choose peace instead. Simply see and know that both you AND the other, by default, are innocent. You, the other, and the world, will certainly be richly blessed!

The Uselessness of Guilt and Shame

As children, very few of us have escaped the pressures of guilt and shame used by our caregivers to control our behavior. Even though it has been a society norm for ages, it is an extreme form of manipulation and falls under the category of abuse! In all types and levels of schooling, this has served as a primary motivation factor to control behaviors and grades, mastered by teachers and parents alike.

Probably the most insidious use of guilt is glossed over in most of our churches where it is used to give the church authority and control. We have so solidly bought into it, that most of us don't even realize how blatantly we have been, or are being manipulated by the church.

Guilt and shame have become a major disease of our society. Guilt has become so accepted and pervasive, that we even perpetrate it on ourselves, believing that we SHOULD feel guilty, for whatever reason.

Guilt and shame are a major cause of low self-esteem in people in most societies. As it is passed on to others, it keeps us in a state of disharmony and mistrust, along with a good dose of either suppressed or expressed anger.

Let's factor in how it has negatively produced the following debilitating core beliefs in the subconscious mind of many people:

- I'm not good enough.
- I am a bad person.
- I will never amount to anything.
- I can't ever get it right.
- I don't belong here.
- I don't deserve to be happy.
- God doesn't love me.
- Other:

Guilt and shame are a man-made ego phenomena, and NOT of God and love. Today make a committed effort to completely let go of guilt and shame. Give it back to the ones that gave it to you and say thanks, but no thanks, and make amends to the ones you hurt with it. Stop putting guilt trips on yourself as well. Eliminate the words "SHOULD" and "SHOULDN'T" from your vocabulary. As each of us makes these changes, we change the world! May God richly bless you on your path to freedom.

Control or the Peace of God?

All wars, whether a war between nations or a war within relationships, are caused by either groups or a single person wanting to control, dominate, or possess others and an insane need to be "right" about everything and making others "wrong". For now, we will focus only on how control affects personal relationships.

Demanding that people acquiesce to our wants and perceived needs very seldom works, therefore we may, out of desperation, try more insidious and covert ways to control others. One such way is through guilt and shame. Another is through fear and threatening, or even cruel or violent behavior. Other ploys are withholding money, things, privileges, or love from another. Others use the threat of abandonment. Some women even attempt control by withholding sex from a mate. None of these will ever work and they usually bring up anger and resentment in another, which is why many intimate relationships fail. When you are consumed with controlling another, your life is one of a constant tug-of-war, attempting to coerce another to play a part that you alone have assigned to her or him. We attempt to selfishly take from them their God-given tree will and power and replace it with ours. This may work for a while, but always culminates in suffering, anxiety, and discord for both parties. This is NEVER God's will and is devoid of true love and caring for another and It will never lead to the peace and happiness we all desire.

A less obvious form of control is when we seek to control the world around us instead of choosing WHAT IS. This is a monumental undertaking and robs us of lots of energy and never really works in the end.

It is much easier to simply surrender all our affairs, problems, and decisions to the Holy Spirit, the comforter and voice for the Father, whose wisdom and love will surely bring the best possible outcomes, ones that engender peace and best serves ALL those concerned. All we have to do in any moment is surrender the ego and ASK and listen for THAT voice, trusting that it will be given. I pray that you trade control for the peace of God!

Examining Honesty and Keeping Your Word

Our world would be so much more enjoyable, loving, and functional if more people were REALLY honest and also kept their word. True, we cannot change others, only ourselves, so let's start there. Even though not lying is fundamentally important, it is not where honesty ends by any means. There are many levels of honesty that we can take a serious look at:

- Leaving out pertinent information is no different than lying and is considered manipulative and dishonest.
- True integrity is when what we think, what we say, and what we do are not conflicted.
- True honesty is when we can look at our own thoughts, words, and actions and admit we have some work to do, without projecting our guilt onto others (making them wrong). Jesus said it so well when he said, "Take the log out of your own eye before you take the mote out of your neighbor's".
- Paramount is being up front about how you think and feel, even when it may feel vulnerable, or may even be unacceptable to others. Remember, honesty is not a matter of being liked or popular.
- Keeping your word is not just honest and the right thing to do, but directly affects your self esteem. It's impossible to care for and love yourself when you can't even trust yourself to do what you say you will. Your word, simply stated, is just as important as making an emphatic promise. Keeping your word will bring more trust and harmony into your relationships.

Take honesty to a new level and watch your life shift to a more gratifying and honorable place! Help to bring heaven on earth, for it is time and YOU are the one!

Relieving Stress in Your Life

Stress causes mental imbalance, addictions, frustration, chaos, anger, depression, and bodily dysfunction, including disease. Your body is truly the temple of God, therefore treat it as such by stoping the abuse. Stress directly and negatively affects relationships too, and should never be taken lightly.

One could say that the the four bottom line causes of all stress are: daily upsets, making something more important than it really is, unmet expectations, and taking on more than is reasonable for one person to handle. Here are some practical ways to avoid stress:

- Avoid attempts to control or fix people, love all unconditionally, continually accepting "what is".
- Determine what is for you to do and what is not. Avoid any need to prove yourself to you or anyone else by doing more or being more than is necessary.
- Balance your time with work, play, and alone time, leaving time for your spiritual practice.
- Be kind and loving in ALL your relationships; make another's interest your own and avoid judgment.
- Remember that you are never stressed out because of an event or any person. You are stressed only

because of how you think ABOUT it. You can always change your thoughts to ones that don't hurt you.
- List other ways which could work for you:

Replace Judgment with Acceptance

Many of us have the habit of judging others. Commonly by:
- How people look, walk, dress, or their mannerisms
- If they have different beliefs or ideas
- If they don't drive the right car, wear the right clothes, have the right hair style or makeup, have the right hygiene, or have the right stuff
- They don't say it right, they are:
- Too quiet
- Too bossy
- Too loud
- Too talkative
- Too self centered
- Too arrogant
- Too wimpy
- Too proud
- Too religious
- Too political   (Add your own.)

Notice when you point your finger at others (judging) you have 3 fingers pointing back at you. Think about it. The worst part though, is that it is impossible to judge and at the same time be peaceful and happy.

Creating Healthy Personal Boundaries

Let's start out by defining co-dependence. It is excessive emotional or psychological reliance on another, even when it is counter-productive. This occurs when one keeps another dependent on them, even if it does not serve the other. This is typically seen in parent-child relationships and when a spouse has a drinking or drug problem; the enabler is constantly saving the dependent other from experiencing the natural consequences of his behavior, thence an opportunity to learn and grow from it. This is not done from a loving, giving stance, but from a selfish motive of wanting to be needed or admired. With that said, at some point, the dependent person may painfully become aware, and in a quest to let go of the enablers influence, must set boundaries for himself to break free of this   dysfunctional relationship by saying to the enabler, "Thanks, 'but no thanks", by direct confrontation. Of course, this chain can also be broken if and when the enabler gets a glimpse of what harm he is doing and simply refrains from the behavior. Either way it will be win-win for both.

An important way to establish personal boundaries with others is to say what you mean and mean what you say. This tool can be used especially, but not exclusively, when parenting children. Of course you will have to give up the need to always be liked. On the positive side, you will be respected more and simultaneously acquire more self-respect . You will always be in integrity when your thoughts, feelings, words, and deeds are not conflicted.

Always saying "yes" to everyone and allowing people to use you for a doormat is another way to give away your power. Therefore we must establish boundaries that communicate to the world that we are not willing to be used and abused. You can learn to say "no" in a loving way, but still mean it.

This doesn't mean that we can't be helpful to family, friends, and even strangers. The trick is to set limits based on our own needs, feelings, and personal limitations. It means saying "no" when it is NOT yours to do, and never saying "yes" just to please someone.

The side effects of giving too much are feelings of resentment and stored up anger, so don't fall into this trap. Avoid people's manipulation and guilt tactics to gain obedience to their demands. Be willing to end relationships where you are not respected and honored, but do it lovingly. There ARE nurturing relationships out there for you. Always remember who you are, a perfect and deserving child of God.

Exploring Authentic Compassion

Compassion is not pity, is not sympathy, is not empathy, and is not kindness, but will contain any or all of these four components. Compassion is "love in action", an active desire to alleviate another's suffering. Nonetheless, let's explore what that phrase actually means. Altruism may help to sum it up. Altruism can be defined as an individual performing an action which is at a cost to oneself, but benefits another, without the expectation of reciprocity or compensation. The compassionate action may expend on your own pleasure and quality of life, along with your time, talents, or even money.

It is not enough to just think about compassion, or know all about compassion, or even feel compassionate, because it is not the same as BEING compassion or BEING an altruistic person.

Compassion and TRUE empathy does not mean joining another in his suffering, for then you are teaching yourself and the other that suffering is real and not just an illusory state of mind. To further explain this: God did neither create suffering nor in any way expect us to suffer, therefore it is not real.

An example of compassion may be as simple as giving the time to really listen to one's story and asking for the feelings experienced within that situation, and being understanding, loving, kind, and reassuring. Often you will be guided to fill a perceived need, whether it be material or just offering some guidance or physical help.

Always be alert to other's sufferings and needs and follow through with true compassion. The more that you love all unconditionally through compassion, the more you will be richly and abundantly blessed with joy, happiness, self love, and general well-being! No matter what you bring to another, the gift returned to you is always incorporated IN THE GIVING!

Anger is Never Justified and Always Hurtful

Anger, as we know it, is the product of negative energy that has built up in the subconscious and conscious minds. It is stored resentments and is usually based on perceived victimizations and judgments of the past. Any experience of anger, whether it be mild frustration or intense rage, and anything in-between, is NOT an expression belonging to the son of God, and need not be a part of our lives. On top of that, it causes stress, separation, disharmony, and disease. Think about that!

Anger is often used to control others, which is both manipulative and dishonest. It may seem to work for some, but all negative energy expressed has its consequences; well known as the universal law of karma.

Anger towards another is never justified and is never for the reason you think. Anger is usually always a reaction of unhealed hurts and beliefs of the past that have been triggered and then show up in the present as anger or hurt. So instead of pointing your finger at the one or the circumstance that you think caused your anger, see it as only a sign that you have healing work to do. My upset worksheet, "Healing my Emotional Wounds of the Past", is designed just for that. Letting go of anger helps you AND the world, to beautifully transform.

Addictions and the Remedy

An addiction is any compulsive and harmful need for something on a regular basis that takes precedence over most everything, even one's health and mental well-being. Common addictions are drugs, alcohol, food, sex, work, shopping, anger, money, power/control, and gambling.

Addictions are a way to cover up feelings, fears and insecurities, but are actually a replacement for God, our good, and border on self-loathing.

Many times one will give up an addiction only to replace it with another, never healing from the real problem, which is the unhealed negative thoughts, beliefs, and fears of the past. Some of these are deeply buried in the subconscious mind. (See my upset worksheet.)

If an addiction is really a replacement for God, then it follows that the remedy is returning to God. God is love and compassion, including unconditional love for self and all others. This includes loving yourself and being truly helpful, kind, and caring to all others, bringing the best out in them. It means viewing all, and yourself, as innocent children of God. It means the absence of being judgmental, defensive, angry, jealous, condemning, competitive, or slandering. If you are loving and giving to this degree, you will be filled with so much joy, love, and peace, that you will never again need anything or anybody to make you feel better, worthy, or complete. Take a walk in this Light and you will never return to a needy, separated, fearful, and addicted way of life ever again.

Harm by Omission

It came to me that I must write on this important subject that is mostly overlooked by spiritual seekers, including myself. Does the title give you a hint of the matter I will be sharing with you?

How many times have we held back our love from others when it could have made a difference? How often could we have said a kind word or even physically helped another, but we were too busy with our lives. Or was it not even apparent that we had an opportunity to lovingly, in some small way, make a difference? Is it cumbersome to say "I love you" to friends, family, and even strangers? It could be simply a sincere smile or a compliment that would brighten one's day! There is always pain and discontent around us, thus an ongoing need for our love and kindness. Have we chosen to walk around blind to the needs of others? How often are we so fixed on just moving from point A to point B, that we fail to love, care for, and even acknowledge the ones we are interacting with.

Whenever anyone is unhappy, sad, in pain, or struggling in any way, they need our love. In truth we are all one so why should it matter if we are very close to that person, or if it is a perfect stranger? When we miss the opportunity to serve another, in whatever way, we are actually doing both of us an injustice. Why? Because when I miss an opportunity to show kindness to another, I have suspended my own very gift in that missed opportunity, the gift of giving. (I always feel really good and blessed after helping another.) At the same time I've blocked the healing that person could have experienced from the interaction. That is what I term a lose-lose situation!

So from this time on, why not commit to staying aware of every moment of every day when you could make even a small difference in another's life, and in your own for that matter. You will, for sure, have left this world in a better condition than before, and your rewards will be bountiful.

Pleasure and Happiness, or Joy?

The feelings of joy, pleasure, and happiness are often deeply confused by many. Pleasure or happiness are temporary experiences resulting from external events in the world. They can be experienced either by something anticipated or something manifested; it can even be experienced by a belief in something that has no real existence, or never transpired. In many cases, it could even be detrimental to one's well being. Common examples of these events could be sex, purchases or gifts that you value, a new relationship or marriage, a pet, a raise in salary, a new job, a diploma, a healing, or even food and entertainment.

Joy, on the other hand, cannot be experienced through pursuing happiness and pleasure. It is a non-fleeting, blissful, internal experience that is reflected from an enlightened state of consciousness. It is the product of an open, loving, and thankful heart and mind. It never relies on any worldly conditions, but transcends all conditions; even disease, poverty, or any loss. Unending peace and joy does comes with a price:

- Nonresistance to the daily experience of the world's challenges and outcomes.
- Having unconditional love of God, self, and all people.
- Service and generosity, making another's interest your own. Being free of all illusions of separation.
- Being non-judgmental, undefended, and non-controlling.
- Being in a constant state of gratitude, kindness, and forgiveness.
- Avoiding gossip and staying in integrity (what I think, say, and do is in alignment).
- Committing to a spiritual path.

This is not to say that pleasure needs to be avoided, but with the absence of joy, you will never fully experience all that God intends for you. So which do you choose, just an occasional temporary fix, or an ongoing state of ecstasy? Choose joy!

The Importance of Daily Quiet Time

I purposely did not want to scare anyone away by using the word meditation, because it means different things to different folks, and many have attempted certain meditation practices without success, and therefore have a resistance to it. It is not necessary to do formal meditation that requires a certain posture, a certain focus, and a certain result. Everybody doesn't want or need that, so just do what you are comfortable with. You don't need to use special words or a special mantra, you can just relate to God or your guides as friends and confidants, for that is truly what they are. I do stress daily quiet time though. Why? Healing of the mind and body can and will take place and stress will be relieved. Most of us get caught up in life's fast pace and we are prone to forget what is REALLY important, and that is our relationship and connection to the Father, our Creator. Without God in our life, we can't feel totally alive and fulfilled. It is imperative that we honor the Holy Spirit, our true self, and our guides by asking for guidance, then listening and accepting the guidance we receive, and giving thanks. Of course, God may be recognized as the Holy Spirit, our Higher Self, Father, Creator, All Knowing, Spirit, Love, or any name you wish to use. What is vital is that we maintain a connection to our Source. You may find it advantageous to use my, "A Prayer to Start Each Day" to set the mood. When you maintain daily uninterrupted, spiritual quiet time in your daily life, you will be richly rewarded.

Disease and Healing

Even though we know that disease is not real (God did not create it.), it must be reckoned with while here in this life. It is now widely known that our thoughts, based on our beliefs, create our reality. The body's affliction is but a symptom of the cause, our flawed and muddled minds.

Worry and stress are serious culprits, which are caused by trying to usurp God's work into our own hands.....Think about this. Surrender and letting go of pseudo control is the solution. Negative emotions, thoughts and beliefs, even the belief in disease, are more destructive to the body than any known toxins.

Our bodies are entirely capable of keeping the body well and disease free. This includes cancer, heart disease, diabetes, arthritis, or anything else. Unfortunately we have bought into the mass fear, mesmerism, and hysteria of suffering and disease, drugs, and the medical community. We have even bought into the idea that we must endear pain and suffering as we age. We even have the crazy and compulsive fear of germs. We are fed these ideas through the TV and other media, especially when the drug companies are bombarding you with fear, in hopes for their bottom line. They don't tell us that their drugs destroy our natural antibiotics that maintain health and heal the body. Did you know that half of our modern diseases only showed up AFTER the advent of deadly commercial antibiotics? Did you know that immunizations by inoculations are toxic to the body and can be deadly? They sometimes even bring on the disease they are supposedly preventing!

As a society, we treat doctors like gods, instead of counting on our own internal wisdom. A case in point..... Our body has normal cancer cells that the immune system is always eliminating. It is only when the immune system is compromised, that it becomes a disease. But you go to the doctor and he tells you you have cancer and have so long to live, he plants that fear and image into your mind, and lo and behold, you aqueous to his spoken word and die, right on time, a self-fulfilling prophecy. He gets his check from your insurance company and he's a happy camper. Even if you are among the few that takes his toxic drugs and gets better, you will succumb to the illness again if you continue with the same debilitating thoughts, emotions, and beliefs.

There are other important thoughts and emotions that affect our immune system, which includes anger, hate, resentment, guilt, shame, judgments, or any other negative thought that takes us out of our peace. The law of karma follows...... What ever goes out, comes back to either bless you or hurt you. In other words, the state of our bodies are a direct reflection of our minds and hearts. Therefore it is imperative, at any and every moment of every day, to clean up our thoughts and live in love of self and others, and to resist nothing. We surrender the body to the mind of God, knowing that Divine order will be established the more we let go of control. We are NOT helpless; we've just not used our God-given power to heal. We were never meant to suffer in any way. So whenever you experience fear of the body or fear of anything, choose the wisdom of God, who is always holding out His love and healing for us.

The only way to reverse and heal from any disease is to get at the root cause and quit seeing the body as the problem. The body is neutral, but at the same time very intelligent. It can't get sick without the prompts from your mind, but yet has full capacity to heal itself and stay well, when given the opportunity.

To learn more, I strongly suggest that you both read and re-read, "Of Monkeys and Dragons", by Michele Longo O'Donnell, or purchase the audio book beautifully read by the author. She enters into great detail on this subject. She and others, including Jesus and Joel Goldsmith, have lived and shared this powerful process of healing. They even demonstrated how others have healed from serious diseases when in their presence. Joel's wonderful book is, "The Art of Spiritual Healing". Delay not in the using of this knowledge, and make a concerted effort to stay well and happy. You will no longer have a need for doctors, hospitals, drugs, and health insurance, which more times than not, are harmful, and seldom have your best interest in mind anyway. Look at all the money you will save! Remember, human solutions NEVER work. Read Wayne Dyer's book, "There is a Spiritual Solution to Every Problem". Another great book is "The Spontaneous Healing of Belief", by Gregg Braden. Above all, remember that God loves you beyond measure and wants you free of disease forever. Honor and glorify God by being ONLY what He created, His beautiful, innocent, perfect, whole, and complete child. Plant your mind on all the love and beauty in the world and all the things to be grateful for, let go of all negativity, and you will be abundant with great health! Be sure to read the section on "Maximal Healing" from Jesus.

Healing with True Forgiveness

Forgiveness, according to "A Course in Miracles", is the relinquishment of believing another can hurt you and forgiving yourself for judging and condemning another for what they didn't do. As you see another, you see yourself. This means that we, all of us, are in truth, innocent, therefore we can never be a victim and there are no perpetrators. We can't change how God created us!

Can you imagine what healing affects can be generated by this idea? Being that all disease and suffering is a direct manifestation of our thoughts and beliefs, we can experience complete healing of the body and emotions by just changing what we hold in our minds. Whenever we have negative thoughts of another, we have traded God's peace for stress, unrest, and suffering. Let's choose peace!

Attachments Hurt Us

If you are attached to outcomes, that is you want and expect things to turn out exactly as you planned or subscribed to, then you are asking for a world of hurt. Be flexible and know that the Holy Spirit, your divine Self, may have a better idea, one that gives you what you REALLY need, even though it might appear to be a little painful or uncomfortable.

Likewise, if you are attached to ANY thing or person you are indeed asking for trouble. For instance, if you are attached to someone and you think they shouldn't leave or die, you will surely suffer if and when they do. Attachment to cars, houses, money, etc. is another road to despair. Another common, but less obvious one, is being attached to how you consider another should act or what they should say.

There is a famous Zen saying, CHOOSE WHAT IS, that would be a constant motto for us all to follow. Choosing (wanting) something different than WHAT IS, will never, and can never be a means of peace and happiness. This idea, implemented, can and will change your life, guaranteed! Let go and let God.

Living Out Your Drama

We all, since our time of birth, have accumulated many experiences that have greatly affected our personalities and who we think we are. From these experiences, we bought into certain fears, core beliefs, and world views, most of them being anything but self-serving. Until we realize that there might be a better way, we are continually, day by day, playing out our life based on these misperceptions. We will call this your story, your drama.

Note which core beliefs below may be yours:
- It is not a safe world; I can't trust anyone.
- I am unlovable

- My body isn't good enough.
- People just want something from me.
- I'm not good enough; I'll never amount to anything.
- Life is hard, and certain ones get lucky or prosperous.
- I am powerless…………I am a victim.
- I'm not smart enough…………..I lack education.
- I will get old and sick………….Suffering is inevitable.

Now take some time in deep contemplation to list some of your own. Go ahead and write them down.

The good news is, by bringing these forward and looking at them, you can make a decision about whether you want to keep playing out this drama or possibly creating new ideas that bring you peace, happiness, and well-being. You have taken the first step in acknowledging what you old thoughts, beliefs, and world views are. Now list some new ideas that will counter your old thoughts and beliefs:

You are on the road to a much better life. Freedom and blessings await you!

Grief and Loss

Everything in this world, other than God's love, is temporary and fleeting. Change is a given, that we can surely depend on. Only when we resist change and loss will we suffer. What this means is this: If we want to live a peaceful and charmed life, we must, in our minds, be constantly and diligently letting go of everything and everyone. We then can see change and loss as an opportunity rather than being victimized by it. God did not intend for us to suffer and grieve. Our will is actually God's will too. In other words, by our natural inheritance, we were not intended to be out of God's grace, EVER. It was only through society's conditioning that we bought into suffering as a normal occurrence. We must change our minds about this and assume full responsibility for our happiness and well being. We can, with earnest diligence, change our minds from fear to love and get back to our original innocence.

To do this, we only focus on the love of God daily until that becomes more important than anything else. You see, holding on to people or anything else, including our money and trinkets, thinking they should never change or go away, is actually an addiction, and all addictions are a replacement for God, it's that simple! Today I want only God (love) so that I will be free! This world means nothing; it is totally fleeting, as is everything in it. Here today, gone tomorrow! I am ONLY here to be truly helpful, nothing more and nothing less. I choose this love rather than fear.

Irrational Thoughts and Beliefs

Our thoughts and beliefs do, in a huge way, affect our lives! Your emotions are directly linked to what you are thinking and believing. Some negative emotions are constructive and others are destructive. Destructive ones are: anger, guilt, depression, shame, hurt, jealousy, embarrassment, and anxiety. Anytime you encounter an upset with any of these emotions, you have work to do.

Here are some typical irrational thoughts and beliefs, with counters to them:

- I am not deserving. I am flawed and I will never be good enough. Counter: I am made by, and am part of the perfect love of God and am sustained by that love. That is the truth and anything I believe that is counter to that is a lie, made up by man, usually used to manipulate and control another.

- If somebody is upset with me, it's my fault. Counter: People get upset based on their own thoughts and beliefs. I stay at peace, no matter what is thrown my way.

- Life isn't fair. Counter: I am responsible for my own life, based on what I think and believe ABOUT it. I love life and it loves me.

- People should treat me better. Counter: I am responsible for taking personally what people say and do. I am invulnerable.

- They have no right to do this to me. Counter: I cannot control people or events, therefore I will choose love and what is, with no need to change anything. I choose peace over stress and strife.

- I never have enough money. Counter: God is my sustenance and I trust in God to provide my needs. (Focusing on lack brings more lack.) I am abundant.

- I am powerless over the government and the power elite. Counter: My power comes from the love of God. I choose love in every moment, instead of fear. I am not a victim and I let go of all fear thoughts.

- I always get sick this time of year. Counter: I let go of debilitating thoughts of suffering. I am perfect, whole, and complete, just as God made me. I only get sick when my mind is conflicted.

Add yours:

A common and debilitating belief is the presence of good and evil, two forces, either working for us or against us. Did you know that God is only good and there is no devil or evil force to recon with? But as long as we believe this, you can never be free or truly happy in your life. This idea has been perpetuated in our churches and from most people in the world, but it is totally flawed. The good news is, you can let go of its mighty grip by simply changing your mind!

You must change your beliefs before you can change your thoughts. in your belief databank, you carry many limiting beliefs that you have picked up from the masses, that have kept your real power hidden from you. In each of us, there is a deep aliveness that has nothing to do with our history or anything else. When you touch THAT, you will be liberated from the small sense of self. You are NOT the body or your intellect, as these are always in flux. You are Spirit, God incarnate. You are free and limitless!

I invite you to go to this page whenever upset and take a good look at what you are believing and thinking and the corresponding fear, pain, and suffering it is causing, and take notes. Remember that you don't have to believe every thought that arises in your head. Just be the awareness that observes the thought. For more on this important subject, I strongly recommend Gregg Braden's book, "The Spontaneous Healing of Belief". It is also available as an audio book.

Prosperity in Giving

Giving may seem like losing something or having less, but actually it is the high road to an abundant life. If you give freely and unconditionally of your time, talents, and treasures, you are assured to live a prosperous and fulfilling life. The reason is that giving IS the receiving. It not only feels good to give from the heart with no strings attached, but at the same time you effect the law of karma which states: For every action there is a reaction. Every time you give something or do something for another or a group, that deed is entered into an invisible bank of the universe and sits there waiting for an opportunity to give back to you in unexpected ways and in the time which is most appropriate for you. This law never fails! So let's talk about ways you can give:

- To your church or any organization that feeds you spiritually. A 10% tithe is a good idea and will give much back in abundance. Give only in love, never out of guilt, fear, or expectations of others.
- To anybody, even strangers, that is in need of money, help, or solace. If you are unsure how to react to someone's need, just stop and quietly ask the Holy Spirit, your true self, for help and listen for the answer to come to your mind. It may be some loving words, a helping hand, money, or whatever. You will know. (We are all one in Christ, therefore giving to another is giving to yourself.)
- By listening intently to others, making THEIR interest your own. This means being genuinely interested in

what they are sharing and not waiting for an opportunity to interrupt with what you just can't wait to say. Use appropriate questions or comments to clarify or confirm what you hear them say. This is the gift of active listening.

- By being kind, generous and complimentary to family, friends, and strangers. A smile or a thank you is often all it takes to make another feel cared for or loved. Always stay in integrity with yourself; make sure that what you think, what you say, and what you do, is in perfect alignment. By the way, this is a recipe for outstanding self-esteem!

BE the love that God created you to be and you will be richly blessed. Give like it is going out of style! You can't out-give God and loving yourself and all people IS loving God.

The Power of Vulnerability
(includes excerpts from talks by Brene Brown, and from "A Course in Miracles")

We are here on earth for relationship, to connect with our brothers and sisters and with God. The hidden truth is we all want and need intimacy, but to realize true intimacy, vulnerability is imperative, period. It is the path for all people in relationships to find their way back to each other with empathy and understanding. The beautiful side effect of becoming vulnerable is that, by your example, you allow others to drop their fears, change their perceptions, and also become free, which is truly a win-win.

You may be asking, "Why would I want to be vulnerable and expose myself; it seems much too painful?" The answer is: It will change your life in a most profound and freeing way, that you could have never imagined or expected.

Men especially have been raised to believe that vulnerability is a weakness, when in truth it is a courageous and powerful way to be in the world. I assure you, it will bring more joy, more fun, more love, more peace, and even more creativity into your life. Being more honest and open with others will produce a deeper, more fulfilling life for sure. You will fearlessly take your mistakes or misconceptions in stride, rather than defending yourself or feeling bad or unworthy. You will display a new courage to be imperfect and allow others the same freedom, never again projecting blame or guilt unto them. You will have the courage to tell another who you are, what you fear, and what you believe, with an open heart; you will become wholehearted. You will have experienced a kindness and compassion for self that allows you to be yourself just as you are, with no judgments. You will let go of any need to please others. This of course releases you from any need for others to be a certain way, in order to deserve your love.

Let's look at some perceived blocks to vulnerability: Many of us carry shame and fear from our past experiences. This is taught by parents and caregivers, in schools, and even in churches. We were taught that we are flawed and never good enough. We are even taught that it is a dangerous world and you can't trust anyone. Is there any doubt that we feel vulnerable and scared? Ingrained in us is the idea that showing our true self is equal to death. (What if people knew who I really am? I would die.)

The truth is we are all children of God, made in His perfect image. That will always be true and never changes, no matter what you believe or what you have done. Your challenge is to get back to that innocence. Try affirming morning and evening, just before retiring, these affirmations:

- I am as God created me.
- I am unaffected and beyond what others may think of me.
- I am perfect, whole and complete.
- I am magnificent and extraordinary.
- I am abundant and blessed.
- I am good and innocent.

(Please add your own.)

Yes, it is an emotional risk and uncertainty to muster up the courage to begin to be vulnerable, so be easy on yourself and know that your amount of willingness is an accurate measurement of your courage.

Ask for help from the Holy Spirit, your true self. That means surrendering your fear and doubt. A little willingness goes a long way. Avoid the temptation to numb yourself with food, alcohol, drugs, or denial. Remember that when you numb yourself from vulnerability, you also numb your joy, excitement, and other good feelings.

As you let go of your fear of vulnerability, you will be able to see how you shine as the beautiful soul that you are. You will have the power and freedom to put your truth and ideas out there, with no fear of rejection. You will have the willingness and courage to invest in a relationship, a project, or an idea that may or may not work out. You will be willing to be wrong, uncertain, or imperfect. You can say "I'm sorry", and mean it. You can fearlessly be the first to say, "I love you" to another, and say it with your whole heart. You can be passionate about life, but at the same time be unconcerned about how it all works out. You can practice gratitude and lean into joy. You can practice forgiveness and see the innocence of others, even of those who, by their words and deeds, seemed to have negatively affected your life. And those whom you have judged.

In the act of being vulnerable, you actually BECOME invulnerable. Think about that.To be vulnerable is to be truly alive and truly beautiful, for all to see.

Can One Heal Depression?

Depression is the result of being self absorbed along with pretending to be a victim. The way out then, is to love and be useful to others and really care about all people, instead of putting yourself first. One must trade narcissistic behavior for being in service to others. It has been said that giving IS receiving. This means that giving is a joyous event that fills the heart and soul. Therefore joy AND depression cannot coexist simultaneously in the same mind and heart.

Beware though, and don't confuse giving with trading! Trading is giving with the expectation of receiving something in return, whereas true giving is without any conditions. We see numerous illustrations of trading under the guise of giving in our world, especially in romantic love relationships. You have no doubt seen examples of this phenomenon in your own affairs, where love disappears when the lover doesn't get the expected reward.

Now about pretending to be a victim. The reason I used the word "pretending" is that, in truth, there are no victims or perpetrators, but at any time we can CHOOSE to be a victim, depending on our past experiences, beliefs, and world views. In other words, each one of us must take responsibility for what we have created in our lives, based on our particular thoughts, beliefs, and world views which we have bought into. If you were to look deep into what you think is true and valid, you will usually find that most of these fears and beliefs are not everyone's, but uniquely yours, and not based in truth.

So, you CAN, and you may choose to, love yourself enough to change your thinking, and thus trade depression for happiness and maybe even joy. Be blessed and know that you are perfect, whole and complete, just as God created you. Actually pretending that you are less is an attack on God! To learn more, read "A Course in Miracles" or "The Way of Mastery", both channeled by Jesus.

The Gift of Intimate Relationships

Intimate relationship should never be downplayed or taken for granted, because it's value goes way beyond what most believe. It is much more than companionship, marriage, or sex; it is the most important opportunity to learn and grow that life can give us. Growing and becoming more is what life is really about and why we are here. We all opted for this experience, so let's make the best of it! Becoming more, growing in Spirit, is more important than fame, success, money, power, looking good, or any material advancement.

The person closest to you, which you call your intimate relationship, or anyone else that seems to be a source of discontent or challenge in your life, is in fact your finest teacher and most generous. Why? Because no matter what they are saying or doing, they are gifting you with an opportunity to love them just as they are. If you answer "no" to this request, you have failed the test, and you will surely suffer.

Everybody, especially your intimate partner, deserves your love and acceptance, and when you finally get this, your life will transform before your very eyes. When you see all others from the eyes of love, you BECOME love, including love for yourself. Man's only real problem is lack of self love, therefore when you love others unconditionally, your own self-love increases exponentially, so the more you give, the more you receive. This is God's law and it never changes.

Love holds no disharmony, no resentments, no judgments, no anger, no guilt, no fears, and no defensiveness. Instead, it brings to the surface acceptance, forgiveness, generosity, kindness, gratitude, joy, peace, fulfillment, harmony, and well being,

As you change your mind about what relationships are really for, your life will magically transform before your eyes. Blessings on you as you open your mind and heart to real love in intimate relationships!

Accepting All of Me

I accept myself completely, with my strengths AND my weaknesses. I accept that I am God's creation dreaming that I am limited to this temporary, illusory world. God didn't make any junk, therefore I have always been perfect and innocent.

I accept that I am here to learn and grow and that I AM doing just that. I accept the personality that I developed, along with its shortcomings. I accept all of myself, unconditionally and without reservations. I know that the core of my being is goodness and that my essence is love, even though I sometimes forget that, and do unloving things. In this unwavering acceptance of myself I find a deep inner strength which gives me the ability to love life and openly accept its challenges so that I might learn and grow from them.

I accept that within my mind are both fear and love, and when I have chosen fear, I always have the power at any moment to choose again. I accept my mistakes as part of growth, so I am always willing to forgive myself and give myself another chance.

I accept that my life is an out-picturing of my thoughts and therefore I commit to aligning my thoughts more and more each day with thoughts of love and innocence, while also forgiving myself when I think unloving thoughts. I accept my life as a blessing and a gift and I am grateful. I stay open to receive and share these gifts freely, with joy in my heart.

How to Be More Loving

Catch yourself judging another, and instead look deep inside of him until you can see the Holy essence in him. Feel that love and notice that it is the same love you have inside of you. Then ask the Holy Spirit, "What is needed here? How can I best serve this person or this situation?" When it is shown to you, have the courage to act on it.

Give a simple smile, a hello, or a compliment when you meet a so-called stranger, even a scary one. Talk as you would to a friend. Affirm in your mind their beauty and perfection. Go out of your way to help the one"s in need. Put yourself in the other's shoes and seek ways to be truly helpful. Give generously of your time, talents and treasures, with no thought of recompense or glory. Practice giving anonymously. Listen carefully to others, even if they appear mundane and boring or seem to have nothing of interest to offer you. Don't attempt to change anyone. Allow others to have their own thoughts, beliefs, feelings, and opinions, even if they are in opposition to yours. Eliminate gossip. Either verbally, or in your mind, send love and blessings to someone who is suffering physically, mentally, or emotionally. Empathize with one who is cranky, ill, or just having a bad day. Do random acts of kindness like paying the toll for a car behind you, buying coffee or lunch for a stranger, taking one's tray up in a restaurant, opening doors, giving your place in line to the person behind, offering money to one who looks needy, or helping the disabled. Have good highway manners, even when others don't. Share your love. Be kind and gentle to yourself and it will reflect on others. Eliminate getting overloaded and out of balance; others will pay the price.

After a time, kindness will become natural and blessings will flow in!

I Am Affirmations of Truth

I am perfect, whole, and complete, just as I am.
I am God incarnate. I am the love of God.
I am the divine light of the world.
I am sustained and supported only by the love of God.
I am patient, loving, and kind.
I am meek and gentle.
I am extraordinary, a unique expression of God.
I am blessed.
I am wisdom.
I am abundant and generous, the heir of God's bounty.
I am fearless.
I am perfect health, perfect strength.
I am the awakened Christ.
I am good and innocent.
I am immortal spirit.
I am joyful and content.
I am unlimited co-creator with God.
I am one with all.
I am perfect relationship.
I am grateful.
I am youthful and energetic.
I am magnificent, capable, and loving.
I am worthy and valuable.
I am a sacred spiritual being with a purpose.
I am lovable.
Add your own:

My Visualizations of Truth

- I am totally filled with God's divine love, preceding my personality. I am always loving.
- Unlimited power of my thoughts and words to manifest now.
- I make all decisions with the Holy Spirit and follow His prompts.
- My memory is crystal clear.
- I can transport my awareness and my body.
- People are healed in my loving presence.
- I can eliminate all pain and bodily dysfunction. My body functions well on very little food and has unlimited strength and energy.
- I defy aging; I experience reverse aging.
- I can send and receive telepathically, even from the spirit world.
- My perception and discernment are very keen and are aligned with love.
- I receive right answers to my questions when asked.
- I serve in greater and greater capacity.

List yours, and be creative and daring:

What is the Holy Spirit and How Can We Access this Wisdom?

With excerpts from"A Course in Miracles"

When we left the side of God eons ago, He gave us the Holy Spirit so we wouldn't lose our way back. The gift of Holy Spirit is actually our right mind, the part of us that is all loving and wise and always connected to God. Since He also gave us free will, we can choose to utilize this power whenever we are ready, whenever we have had enough of pain and suffering.

So, to move through this world with ease, it behooves us to call on this wisdom and make it our friend, our best friend! We can daily turn over to the Holy Spirit all problems, all circumstances, and all decisions and get answers based on love and healing for all concerned. The only thing we must let go of is the ego (Edging God Out) that thinks it can do it alone, and surrender to a higher Source. Here is a systematic procedure to accomplish this in the midst of everyday life:

First we must decide that there is a better way. We must be willing to change, and want more than anything else, to experience the peace of God, which brings joy, love, and well being. We must give up the need to be right, give up judgements and condemnations of self and others, and have a pure heart. That means loving all unconditionally, no matter what they appear to be doing or saying.

The rest is simple but not always easy, so practice is essential. It involves stopping in any moment, putting your mind at rest and asking Holy Spirit for guidance and then be willing to listen and wait for that guidance in the way it comes for you. This may include an inspired thought, a dream, a message from another person or source, or even audible words in your mind. If you allow ego to enter in, the answer won't feel peaceful nor beneficial to all concerned.

So, just stay willing as much as possible to receive help from the Holy Spirit which resides not outside of you, but within. When patiently asked, the Holy Spirit will always show you another way to look at your situation, through the eyes of love. Help is always just a decision away! All that's required is the trust and willingness to receive divine intervention. Don't cheat yourself by thinking you only need to consult the Holy Spirit on very important matters! With this, I welcome you to a happy, fulfilled life.

Message from a Loved One Who Passed

I know that you think I have left you, but I am really just a thought away! I am home now and you will be joining me soon in this realm of unspeakable beauty and unconditional love. This love that I feel here was always on the earth plane, I just wasn't aware of it. So abide in that love now and allow it to comfort and console you, to heal and restore you, and bring laughter and joy during your difficult moments. I can assure you that your world is just an illusion, a dream, and when your heart is filled with love, the world will just fade away into the nothingness it came from. All the obstacles you have encountered in your life are all gifts given you to heal your mind and heart. The challenge of my passing is no different, so be thankful unto the Lord because the universe is conspiring on your behalf!

Until we are reunited, be vigilant in your work and let go of the past, including me, and set your sights on YOUR homecoming while you love yourself and everyone unconditionally, so that you can feel the same bliss that I experience now.

I now know that heaven on earth was always possible for all. The good news is that you don't have to wait until you enter the next dimension. We are all gods, but in different realities! So live your life as though it is a blessed event. All that happens is either for your pleasure or your growth, and they are both good if you don't resist either. Let your light shine in the world and you will be richly rewarded. I will prepare for your homecoming of celebration and ecstasy as you discover your true divinity, as I have in my new home.

What Enlightenment Is and Isn't
Excerpts taken from "A Course in Miracles" and writings by Gary R. Renard

Enlightenment is the absolute transformation to the constant state of being totally in the now, where I know without a doubt, that I am the manifestation of God and that we are all one; that there is only one thing in this world that matters.....the expression of love. It is an awareness that each and every one of us is already perfect, whole, and complete, just as we were created, as spiritual beings. It is a state of mind where the world and what's in it just kind of drops away, along with the ego part of our personality. What becomes most important comes to the forefront of our minds which is God and unconditional love for self, everyone, and everything. This is What "A Course in Miracles" calls true forgiveness. You will still be in the world, but not OF the world. You are born anew and your life becomes peaceful and filled with love and joy. You are no longer striving for the things of the world, like money, comfort, entertainment, material things, power, or fame. You cease to be attached to certain outcomes. You will always choose "what is" instead. Your main goal becomes service to mankind and assisting others to obtain the same freedom you have learned to experience. This, of course, can best be done by just showing up as an example of the Christ, as Jesus did 2000 years ago. This is called Christ Consciousness. The result for you is always peace, joy, happiness, and fulfillment.

The Faith that Blesses

Just having faith does not suffice; faith without feeling and action just doesn't cut it. Religious error has spread so thoroughly that many people assume that all that is needed is faith (belief) in Jesus. What Jesus required of us was much more than that. While on the earth, he demonstrated the path to the Kingdom of God (a state of mind, not a place) and promised that we could enter the

Kingdom as he did, while still here on earth. He taught that it was an inside job and that no knowledge, religion, or outer path would grant us an entrance. This means we deny the world and focus primarily on God (love) and forgiveness. It means loving everyone unconditionally, making your brother's interest your own, and letting go of the ego's need to be separate and right. It means giving up judgement, resentments, righteousness, greed, competition, envy, and hatred. It means setting aside the carnal pleasures of the world for something better. It means taking the log out of your own eye instead of the speck from another's. It means being generous with your time, talents and energy, including money. When you do this with faith, and with acceptance of life as it is, then life flows for you, and you will feel the Love, and you will be uplifted.

Remind yourself daily, regardless of how you feel emotionally, and regardless of how dire your circumstances may be, that you are a beloved child of God, being supremely cared for in every moment, and turn to Him with an open heart so that He may fill it with His Love. This is TRUE faith, the faith that continually blesses and allows you to become more. Be vigilant on your spiritual path and you will be blessed beyond measure.

What is the Ego and Why Am I Here?
(with excerpts from Spirit channel, Matt Kahn, and "A Course in Miracles")

Ego is an over-stimulated nervous system. Here is the explanation: Ego is not only the personality, but something that HAPPENS TO the personality that causes it to see things exaggerated, not as they are. The personality becomes inflamed and sick. This happens through the process of being raised in this insane world, and being conditioned into a low level of consciousness that is contrary to our NATURAL state of being. There are four ways the ego is played out, that I'm sure will strike a familiar chord:

1. Righteous inflammation is when you need other people to be wrong for you to be right and feel ok. It not only shows up as self-righteousness, but also as one-upmanship. (e.g. That's nothing, look who I am, look what I know, or look what I can do.)

2. Victimized inflammation is blaming others, God, or self instead of hesitating and using loving discernment to see any situation differently and clearly, from the eyes of love.

3. Entitled inflammation is when you think everything belongs to you, even at the expense of others, and you expect to be served and cared for under all conditions.

4. Needy inflammation is when one never feels heard and never gets enough. ("You never spend enough time with me.", "You don't make eye contact.", "You never give me your full attention.") More subtly they may ask, "Are you

fully present with me?" I call these folks emotional vampires or energy thieves.

Waking up from this dark ego sleep is simply letting go of this inflamed personality and coming back to our true nature, which is love. It's that simple, but it does take a willingness and effort. So, all our individual personalities that we came in with, got infected, like an allergy, and that is recognized as the ego. The good news is, it actually is NOT real because it didn't come from Love and wasn't God's plan.

We are ultimately here to assist in the world's awakening by first putting aside our own egos and then teaching others by our example. Love is who we and all others TRULY are, not egos, so when we experience another in his ego, instead of judging and condemning him, it's an opportunity to see him as sick and suffering, calling out for love. Therefore the appropriate response is to respond WITH love. It is an opportunity to ask the Holy Spirit, your real and higher self, how you can be truly helpful to this brother/sister (who is actually A PART OF YOU). It is an excellent opportunity to show authentic compassion, which is love in action. When people are in their egos and seem to be suffering, give them a compliment or some form of love, as you're guided. The side effect is: YOU are healed simultaneously! Why? Because we are truly one and divinely connected. So BE the light of the world and you will be richly rewarded; there is no better use of time on this planet!

What is Time and Is It Real?

Time, as we know it, was an idea made by man, probably to gain an understanding and some order of the world. Because the world and everything in it, was NOT created by God, it is truly NOT real, with the exception of the love in it. To exemplify this: You can't find God in the past or the future of time, only in the eternal now.

With this said, a useful concept of time is the division of years in months, weeks, and days. This provides us with a calendar, which is certainly beneficial to plan for certain times to do certain things in an appropriate manner. On a daily basis, it helps us to organize our days to meet work schedules, meetings, appointments, bedtimes, eating times, etc.

Then there is a less useful concept of time which divides time into three sections, known as past, present, and future. This idea of time can create many problems for us. You see, there is truly only NOW, therefore the past actually happens IN THE NOW and the future never happened, but is only anticipated in the NOW. Thinking and worrying about the past and future keeps us from fully experiencing the eternal now where God resides.

The past consists of thoughts, images, experiences, and beliefs stored dormant in our subconscious mind, that can and will make havoc for us. "A Course in Miracles" states that we are never upset for the reason we think! What that means is that our upsets are actually triggered by past thoughts, events, and beliefs in our subconscious mind that is totally irrelevant to our NOW experience!

This useful information will dispel the belief that anyone's words or action, or any situation, can really hurt us, or in any way affect us. We can then forgive ourself for our flawed perception and ask the Holy Spirit, our true nature, to help us see it differently from the perspective of NOW, and through the eyes of love. With this new perception, you can and will experience much more peace and joy in your life! Seriously think about this. Please check out the worksheet on "Healing My Emotional Wounds of the Past", designed to bring truth and healing to your upsets.

I suggest you read this each evening before retiring and be as God intended, limitless!

The Attitude of Gratitude

Gratitude is not merely the greatest of all virtues, but the parent of all others. This important segment of spiritual growth is often side-stepped. The truth is that without gratitude, being thankful, your spiritual path cannot be complete. Why? Because without the unceasing prayer of gratitude one does not experience all the beauty and abundance that life has to pour out upon us. Regular engagement in gratitude will heal the mind and help undo the ego. It is impossible, when engaging in gratitude, to simultaneously suffer or be upset. Without the gratitude attitude, one walks around just partially alive. The truth is, the more thankful you are, the more comes your way!

Related to gratitude is appreciation, so if you consistently look for something or someone to appreciate, even in difficult situations, you can expect your life to change for the better. When you are actively attuned to gratitude and appreciation, you will inevitably uncover more of the same for yourself, bringing you so much joy, optimism, peace, abundance, and harmony that you won't have the time or desire to worry or think about anything negative!

Remember though, that silent gratitude isn't much use to anyone. When you actually EXPRESS appreciation to another, it is a double whammy, because then both you AND they are blessed. What you give to another you give to yourself. Why is that? Because we are truly one and NOT separate. When we really get it, not intellectually but experientially, the idea of oneness, love and caring become natural and very healing for all. Service to EVERYONE becomes a way of life and brings much peace and happiness,"When I give to you, I give to myself" becomes more than just a slogan, but becomes truly realized.

Besides the benefit to you, gratitude will also lead to positive and transformative action in the world, just by your modeling of it for others.

Your Spiritual Path

Any spiritual path that has substance will teach unconditional love and forgiveness. It will instruct you to look beyond the world's pleasures and seek God (love) as your #1 priority. Deep transformation and peace will be it's objective. For me, "A Course in Miracles" and "The Way of Mastery" have served me well. Both were given by Jesus through human channels (scribes who heard the voice and wrote what they heard into book form). For years I conscientiously attended groups weekly and was a dedicated student. I had a wonderful intellectual understanding of the material and I could communicate it well. It was not until many years of studying that I finally decided to take steps that would actually incorporate what I had learned into my life as practical experience. It wasn't until then that I realized that my academic spiritual knowledge had produced no life-changing experience. It was the commitment to LIVING the principles that made the real difference. It was the letting go of my old ways and applying what I had learned, that transformed my life in so many beautiful ways.

So I ask you now: Are you on an effective spiritual path and have you experienced a major shift in your life? If not, I encourage you to not waste as much time as I had. Put forward that special effort that will allow you to have the fantastic experience of true peace, harmony, and utter joy. This is the result of giving unconditional love and service to all, along with releasing judgment and condemnation. I would love for you to partake of this experience, if you have not yet. It is very easy to get caught up in laboriously intellectualizing spiritual material while still accepting the status quo of struggling with life, and considering it normal.

Follow what your heart tells you and trust in God's love.

The Power of Love

Love is the only answer to any problem or issue you are dealing with. Deep within each of us is the knowing of this truth. Love is what will open your mind and heart to see things differently, through the eyes of Love. Love is powerful enough to actually change the world if we would only remove the blocks to its presence. It is always a part of us, waiting to be acknowledged. Love and only love heals. No healing modality can work without the love to back it up. This illusion we call our world, is an illusion that we built as a means to experience separation from God and therefore from one another. It has been extremely successful in convincing you that you are a separate, tiny, and insignificant part of an unimaginably vast and threatening whole. The truth is, you have within you the divine Spark of Love from which you were created that is inextinguishable, but which has been hidden from your sight by the cloak of darkness that contains and maintains the illusion. The following is from from Jesus, channelled by John Smallman (JesusthroughJohn.com): Many Dismiss Hope as childish nonsense. You are on the cusp, at the beginning of a new and wondrous way of relating to one another as the tsunami of love continues to intensify and bring into the collective awareness the realization that love is the only way to resolve issues and conflicts, whether between individuals, families, political or religious belief systems, or nations. Wherever you go, leave your heart print! Grow strong enough to love the world, yet empty enough to sit down at the same table with it's worst horrors. Love is your nature, and is at the depths of your essence. Love is joyful, accepting, enthusiastic, comforting, and inspiring, as divinely intended.

When you experience love, you find that it is irresistible, and you realize that is what the vast majority of humanity have been seeking for eons. Love is accepting, enthusiastic, comforting, and inspiring, as divinely intended. You cannot live without love; it is the life force, the limitless field of infinite divine energy, in which All That Is has It's eternal and utterly fulfilling existence. You are alive, and therefore held closely in the warm embrace of the field of love which supports you totally and provides abundantly for all your needs, without you having to, as it were, lift a finger. Love is the life force; you cannot live without it. You are, every one of you, essential parts or aspects of It. However, when you constructed the illusion you attempted to exclude It, by apparently separating yourselves, shutting yourselves off from God. That is not possible, but you were and are free to pretend that it is, and that is what causes you so much pain and suffering. What is the impact of fear on love? Fear is intensely restrictive. Love is infinitely inclusive. The two cannot co-exist, you have to choose between them, and only love is real! So, truly there is no choice, just the requirement that you open your hearts to release your belief in fear, to let it go and refuse to acknowledge it. When you do so, love will flood in, filling the space that fear had occupied, had fenced in, so that your heart center will expand, and you will feel love and see It and recognize it everywhere. Love is your nature, your Source. It is all that exists. And by shutting yourselves off from It you have caused yourselves immense pain and suffering throughout the eons. Having had enough of this insane way of experiencing life, you made the collective decision to awaken, and collectively you most definitely are stirring in your deep slumber, moving positively and inexorably towards the moment of your awakening. It is your hearts which are stirring, because in truth you are all Heart, and it is your hearts that have been so closed off and restricted by the illusion. It is as though you had conned yourselves fearfully within a tiny dwelling, with no windows and only a tiny bolted door through which you could enter or leave, while outside, waiting for you to emerge so that He could embrace and caress you, your Father was watching over you and keeping you eternally safe and secure. To awaken is to unbolt that door and emerge into the brilliant light of eternal day. Love is stable and enduring and has a real effect on all of us. I know, at that level of recognition that is not illusory, that love is all that exists. I know that love is not a part of the hologram, the illusion. Love is the beginning and the end, the alpha and the omega and, if we had the eyes to see, everything in between. There is nothing greater than love.

You can be enamored of the illusion, of the thrill of the chase, of the temporary ecstasy of some things, of the up's and down's and in's and out's, but the only thing that satisfies completely and lasts forever is love. (End of message from Jesus)

Speaking of loving, we must take time to love ourselves, to nurture ourselves, and give ourselves alone time to be with the Holy Spirit, our real Self. Without this self love, you won't become much of a lover of God or man. You can never be too busy to love and nurture yourself; it is that important! Whenever catching a glimpse of yourself in a mirror, just say with feeling, "I love you.", and maybe give yourself a big belly laugh or a hug.

Jesus didn't teach the 10 commandments, he only taught one: Love God, love yourself, and love everyone. This includes the most unworthy person you or the world has ever judged! In the end, we are here only to master relationships, that is to take any adverse situation and respond to it with love. When you perceive an attack by another, know that what they really want and need is love. Therefore respond only with love, instead of judgement, anger, self-righteousness, or defense. Love eradicates the need to be right and eliminates complaining! Love is the most powerful energy there is, so love everything, every circumstance, every person and watch the world change around you. You will have accomplished your part in creating heaven on earth.

Know that whatever shows up in your life is only an opportunity to extend love and your life will change dramatically. Is it not true that we create our own world? So, then create one that is loving, harmonious, joyful, and peace filled. Make love your only genuine priority! Start a love revolution in your own heart today, and do your part in creating a new world for all!

Worshiping God

Do you worship God? Is God an ego that needs to be worshiped to feel OK? Unfortunately most people want to assign God a body (usually male) and give Him a human personality instead of seeing Him as divine love and perfection, our real father, and the creator of all that is.

According to Jesus in "A Course in Miracles", man started to worship God to appease Him and sidestep His perceived wrath because we felt guilty and afraid for leaving His side and choosing to be independent egos. (Ego stands for edging God out.) The answer to this dilemma is simply to go back to God, and be His divine child whom He originally created, perfectly loving, whole, and complete, likened to the Creator Himself. It is only a mere decision away to again surrender to Him for His sustenance, love, peace, and joy.

No church, minister, or guru can do this for you. When will you decide you've had enough suffering? How much pain do you need to endure before you change your mind? Making this decision would mean eliminating judgement, anger, defensiveness, jealousy, needing to be right, and anything else not born from love, but from fear and guilt. So which do you choose, disharmony, pain, and suffering or the unconditional love and peace of God that manifests when you love all unconditionally. If you haven't already, love yourself enough to choose God, to choose love!

What Jesus Said

Jesus did not intend to be worshiped; he wanted to be followed. It is certainly easier to worship him than to follow his teachings. He demonstrated the path to the kingdom of God for us to follow. He taught that finding God was an inside job and that no knowledge, religion, or outer path would grant us entrance into the kingdom of God. The kingdom of God is a state of consciousness, not a place. He taught that we could enter with the Holy Spirit while still here on earth, as he had done.

What this implies is that we become one with God and all his creations (everything and everybody). It means that we deny the world and focus primarily on God and forgiveness. It means letting go of the ego's need to be separate and right. It means loving everyone unconditionally. It means giving up judgement, righteousness, resentments, greed, competition, envy, and hatred. It means joining with your fellow man and making his interest your own. It means setting aside the carnal pleasures of this world for something better. It means taking the log out of your own eye instead of the speck out of your brother's. It means being generous with your time, talents, and energy (including money). Jesus summed it up by saying, Love God, yourself, and everyone with all your heart, with all your mind, and with all your soul. He taught to live life with an open and pure heart as he did. He taught we were born as extensions of God, not as sinners.

His teachings were very radical for the times and have been watered down since. You see, if we worship Jesus and claim He is above us and is God Himself and we are just sinners, then we can rationalize his teachings, by saying only Jesus is that good and pure, thereby absolving responsibility to follow His teachings and becoming LIKE him. Unfortunately, this is what is being taught in many churches today. We are taught that all we have to do is believe in Him and we are saved. Experiencing the peace that passes all understanding, takes a commitment; it takes a deep intention and serious work. It isn't given freely. This is only a portion of the misunderstandings of the teachings of Jesus as taught by Christianity. So much of the truth and light in the Bible is hidden or misinterpreted.

To learn more, check out the book "Maximum Faith" by George Barna, the website: askrealjesus.com, or read either "A Course in Miracles" or "The Way of Mastery". I give this information with heartfelt love and a sincere desire that you transform your life, thus transforming the world, and ultimately bring up attendance in our churches, through the pure teachings of Jesus. It is time, NOW.

My Letter to God

As you know, God, much of my life I was negatively influenced by the world around me. I was taught that the world was a fearful place and I needed to protect and take care of only myself, to not trust people, and to fear You, because You were a judging and condemning god. Even though you gave me free will, You would send me to hell if I didn't live up to your expectations. None of this concern and worry never brought me any peace or joy, but conversely brought me pain and sorrow. I accepted this idea of Life, never really questioning it for a long time. I know now that I was totally and sadly misled. Now I know that I was made in Your image of divine love, a love so pure and unconditional that I have trouble wrapping my mind around it. I need do nothing to receive Your love because it is already in me and will always be part of me because we are one and the same. Jesus showed me if I asked for and accepted this love, it would purify my heart and I would be born anew as an innocent child and would enter Your Kingdom. I just had to let go of the idea that I was separate from others and learn to love everyone and myself unconditionally. I even let go of condemnation and judgment of myself and others. Today my life is extraordinary because I am no longer fearful and I am sharing Your love and my gifts with all people that I meet. I am very peaceful, and so thankful that I found another way to be in the world. I love you God, and I know now that

You were always faithfully by my side, even when I was misguided. I am blessed as Your child!

Laughter is Good Medicine

Ho, Ho, Ho! Lets have a good life and not take ourselves TOO seriously. There is plenty to laugh about. I sometimes look in the mirror and laugh hysterically. I can watch people and quietly laugh at what they do and say, knowing they are all doing the best they can. In my spiritual groups, I think of crazy things to say that get people to laugh or even smile. Children always bring a smile to my face. They are so in the moment and innocent, aren't they? Their spontaneity cracks me up....out of the mouths of babes. When I make a mistake, drop something, break a dish, trip and fall, or whatever, it is always a good reason to laugh at my humanness! I enjoy being around people that help me in this endeavor. Won't you join me, and we'll laugh together?

20 Steps to True Peace and Joy

NOTE: These steps are in no specific order. You may want to work one at a time for a period of 20 to 30 days. Your life is sure to change, and you'll be on the road to an enlightened mind. Excerpts taken from "A Course in Miracles" and askrealjesus.com.

1. I make another's interest my own. I see his suffering as my own; I have a true desire to be helpful. I give selfless service regularly and when appropriate.

2. I judge not another; I take the log out of my own eye, not the speck out of another's. I cannot have the desire to change anyone unless I have first judged him. I give up the belief in dualism (right and wrong, good and bad) that causes judgment. I don't criticize, ignore, or otherwise withhold my love from another. I am patient and calm.

3. I don't engage in or start gossip. Gossip is an attack on both myself and the other. Judging another is always a projection of my own guilt.

4. I stay in integrity. What I think, what I say, and what I do are not conflicted. I always speak my truth and release any need to be liked.

5. I commit to a daily spiritual practice that keeps me focused on God and love. I do my best to avoid distractions such as TV, internet, cell phones, and other potential addictions. I intentionally bring love and caring into all parts of my life.

6. I give up defensiveness (turn the other cheek). I let go of anger and condemnation and instead I see an attack by another as a call for love and then answer the call WITH

love. I let go of the need to be right or to make another wrong. Love is patient and kind.

7. I surrender my personal stories, drama, and beliefs that keep me imprisoned in the past. I am not my "poor me" stories, I am free! I let go of and heal anger, hurts, and resentments that I am harboring from the past. I practice forgiveness daily and surrender the idea that anyone can hurt me.

8. I let go of control, attachments, and outcomes. I always choose what is happening right now, not what I think I want. Only the NOW encompasses God's love and perfection, therefore I choose what is in front of me and make appropriate decisions about it.

9. I forgive myself, God, and all perceived perpetrators for what I think they did, as I change my beliefs and perceptions that led me to that perpetrator/ victim thinking.

10. I practice gratitude daily, even in difficult situations,because I can never see the whole picture or end result. There is always much to be thankful for. I stay humble and rely on God. Gratitude will help to undo the ego and bring me peace.

11. I give up vanity and conceit and a need to be noticed or acknowledged. I give up competition and comparing myself to another.

12. I engage in random acts of kindness, even for strangers and the seemingly undeserving. I am always truly helpful wherever I am.

13. I give up, envy, resentments, hurts, anger, and hatred. Even ignoring another is an attack on them. I cannot envy another if I know our oneness. Everyone deserves my love and respect.

14. I treat all strangers, even the scary ones, as friends. I can look in their eyes and see the same Christ that is in me, and smile.

15. I listen carefully to others instead of planning my response, even to the seemingly mundane and unintelligent, for they deserve my love, and listening IS loving.

16. I am generous with my time, talents, love, possessions, and money. If I see a need, it is mine to fill. Remember, a gift that has any expectations is NOT a gift, it is a trade. I let go of greed. Giving IS receiving!

17. I pay attention to my thoughts, words, and beliefs, for they directly affect my reality. I take full responsibility (not blame) for what I create; I am never a victim. I think only about what I like and want, not what I don't want, so that I

can manifest appropriately. I take whatever steps are necessary to fulfill my intended manifestations.

18. I give over my fears to God. I am not a body, I am Spirit, therefore there is nothing to fear except fear itself. To the Holy Spirit I surrender the fear of death, pain, lack, or loss. I even give up fearing the future. Debilitating fear never again runs my life and overshadows my peace and well being.

19. I have the openness and spontaneity of a child. I have a sense of wonder and innocence. I freely play, sing, dance, and spend time in nature. I observe and interact with children because they are great teachers for me.

20. I give up chasing love, security, pleasures, power, money, and material things. I trust in God's love, bounty, and protection instead. Love and service to mankind is my one and only goal.

A Prayer to Start Each Day
Copy this and place by your bedside
Holy Spirit, this is the day I choose to be a channel for Your divine love. I need not look anywhere for this love because it is my birthright from the Creator. I give to you this

day, to direct my thoughts and actions. Today I will be Your hands and feet, Your voice and ears, Your mind and heart, and I will see through Your eyes of love. I choose to be an open vessel of your love and kindness. Let me be an example to all my brothers and sisters I meet today exemplified by my loving words and deeds. Let me release all judgments and condemnations so I can see in each one their innocence and perfection, as well as my own. With your help, I will see beyond actions and appearances that might offer my mind something different from this truth.

I thank you for your love, caring, and guidance today that will afford me peace, wisdom, abundance, hope and joy. I love God, myself, and every brother and sister on this planet, because WE ARE ONE in truth.

2. Messages from God and Jesus

From God
Sourcing the New World From Within
from God (a channeled message from the internet)

Beloved ones, in these important times I must urge you to remember that your life flows forth from Me. You live from the Spirit outward. Your heart is the entry point for every increment of energy that then becomes your life and everything that you see in it.

Therefore, I ask you to return, daily and even hourly, to that feeling place of perfect faith where you feel the astounding power of this Love -- where you recognize that I Am your daily bread, that I Am your food. First is the spiritual and then it becomes physical. It becomes the symbols of the world.

As your heart opens and your vibration soars, you will find your life coming more into accord with that which your heart knows as the truth. But, dearest ones, don't stop there, and don't be fooled into looking outside of yourself for that which brings you what you need.

Remember that it comes as Love. It comes from Me. The more that you feel and believe this, the more will manifest as a world of beauty, as Heaven on Earth. As you see your life change, and you feel Love urging you to take this action, or that one...please, go ahead. Act on the urgings of the Spirit of Love.

Listen when you hear My guidance. But always be sure to stop for a moment and to be aware from whence your blessings come. Connect to the vibration of Love. Re-establish the continuity, the flow, until every atom of your being remembers that I Am the Source and I Am Love and you are this very energy.

You are My heart. You are My Light, and this communion is the spiritual soil from which every symbol springs, every experience of your life. Especially when you feel powerfully guided to take action, to serve, to embrace a certain path, to imbibe a certain food that speaks to you of vibrant health, remember that it comes from this communion and is made manifest always through your heart.

The human perspective has always been to look outside of yourself and to believe that nourishment comes as food and abundance comes as money. But in the truth of the heart it is clear that the Source is the Moment of Creation. It is the energy of life. It is the power of living Love that is then made manifest to reflect to you the space in which you live, the level of our communion, the blessings of your deep connection to the endless life I Am.

Beloved ones, we are making a shift in this world that means everything. It is the shift to Love. It is the awareness of God. It is the truth of the unity of one life breathing you and living in exuberance here and now.

It is from this place that the New World springs into being, the world that your heart is creating, the vision that has been before you for the whole of your life. It is the conviction within that peace can reign, that equality and abundance is for everyone and that Love is the only truth.

It is now time for these things to be actualized, to be made manifest, to be lived and rejoiced in. But the only way this can be done is if each of you, beloved ones, deeply remembers the Source. You must remember the flow, that all life is sourced through the heart from the glorious explosion of God I Am awakening as Love.

You are an integral part of this by re-establishing your true faith in the source of your life, in the feeling level of the heart and our communion and then, holding this as your truth until it is clear that the life that you live in the world is a result of your heart's attunement.

Look to Me as your bread, your water, as the food by which you truly live and the abundance which supports you...even if at first it feels and seems impossible and flies in the face of everything you have experienced through the mind as your human expression. As you listen, as you pause, as you make the choice to remember to attune to the source of life, to remember first and foremost that it is this place of communion, this trust in our Love, this connection to the circle of life, of Love, of giving that then becomes your world in this moment that you take to remember -- before reaching for the food on your plate, before using that money for a purchase, before making your choices of what needs to be part of your life.

When you hold this vibration of trust in Me, when you look upward for your spiritual sustenance, it brings you into the vibration of the New World, the world that is truly Heaven, the world that is Love made manifest. In every area this is the truth, every area...in areas you have never even paused to consider.

In the area of Love relationships, of course...but in the areas that are seemingly sourced from outside of you such as the garden, the growing of food, the choices of what to eat...even the belief that you must take care of the body in certain ways...all of this I simply ask that you remember to take one moment and to pause, to open your heart, to re-establish the remembrance, the connection to the real flow of life and to send forth a prayer of gratitude that I Am your Source -- for example, that I Am your food, that I Am your energy, that I Am your warmth, your ability to take care of the circle of your life, of your environment.

All of this comes from within, bursting through the heart as the energies of Love, and the results of our communion are then made manifest in the symbols of the world and the life that you are living here. In these times of powerful change, the greatest shift of all is this remembrance that you can look to Me for everything. The Love that you are sustains you.

The more deeply that you feel this and that you believe on the feeling level, on the level of resonance that life comes forth from Me...that you are fully created in limitless glory in the eternal Now Moment, that you can embrace this perfection, say "Yes" to it, say "Yes" to life in ways the mind cannot imagine...then, trust your heart to make manifest this Love, this life force, this joy in the experience of living, as every moment of your experience in the world.

As you connect to Me as the Source of everything, you are more easily freed from the consensual dream of life outside of you. This doesn't mean there is no call to action or that you don't need or want to eat food...although this can change.

It means that when you make the choice, there is a moment of remembrance before you move that re-establishes the actual flow of Real life, of its establishment as the beautiful expression of God you are, here and now. And then, once you feel this remembrance and once there is a song within your heart that knows you are perfectly supported, then make your move. Buy your food. Make your juice. Imbibe in the symbols of Creation as they show up as your world.

If, as yet, some of those symbols are imperfect and are still holding the resonance of duality, first allow the living Spirit to inform you of the gift of service in the experience you are living. Then, re-affirm this life and your connection to Me as the Source, your ability to be this explosion of Love.

Feel your heart as this magnificent sun that pulses forth the energies of God I Am which you live and name and make yours. Hold that feeling state of divine communion as you go forth, and through the heart, connect with everything -- establishing Real communication with the energies of Love that become your world as you keep looking upward and raising your vibration until that which you see is the truth of who you are.

So, beloved ones, at this moment it is like strata. The energies of the New World are high and clear. The energies of the old world are more muddied, confused. They are still tied to the old way of seeing things. Your work if you will is to keep holding to a world of Love that is sourced from God and flows forth through your heart to be made manifest as a world of life and health and abundance of body, of Love, of relationship, joy...abundance work, service, all of it.

It is first brought forth in you, manifested in the symbols of your changing world and then, honored, beloved ones, and this is so important ... honored as the expression of the Love you are, embraced in communion by your heart, and celebrated.

That you might now become a conscious participant in life is the goal. This now is the vision that resonates within you. Trusting this life, this Love I Am, as sufficient for your every need will bring to you your ability to live as the heart of God, open, available and infinitely free...right here, while expressing as a human being.

As your heart opens, the world changes. Relating to this world consciously is important. This means relating to your own heart, that you might stop and remember and honor life and all of its gifts, that Love may be made manifest as the world. The world of Love is brought forth right now through this moment of remembrance and communion, through seeing the Source within your heart and clinging to it, allowing Me to keep feeding you freedom.

In this time you are powerful creators. In this time your heart's beliefs will be made manifest, consciously ameliorated by Love, as long as you acknowledge your heart and live from the inside outward.

Now I have said to you that everything you see is simply a veneer painted on the world of Love – the reflection of the heart's beliefs in separation from your whole and perfect good. This is the truth and the circle does go both ways. You can make this connection with the truth of life, with the Source of Love by moving through the illusion, by taking what you see as the world and not believing it and using your heart to see the truth and to move right through the illusion. This brings you, beloved ones, to the same place.

But because we are healing duality, because it is time to end the belief in separation from Me, from Love, from the glory of the life you are, it is important to now recognize the Source within you and your open heart as the powerful conduit for releasing into the world the true activity of Love, vibrant, alive, full of joy. This will allow you to focus your world, to be the acknowledgement that the Love within you becomes the world you see and that I Am always supporting you.

I Am the fulfillment of your every need. The more that you feel this, the more amazing your life will be, with things that you need showing up in an instant in absolutely amazing ways.

So look to Me when you open your eyes in the morning before you think about what must be done for the day. Before you think about the weather or what you shall be wearing, return to your heart and bathe in Me until you remember that every good and all that you need is supplied, and through your heart, even the weather changes and abundance will seem to drop from the sky or show up in ways you can't foresee.

Even in the simple things, remember that your life comes forth from Me. As the Moment of Creation births anew the wholeness of Love as the hologram, feel the resonance of this truth. Then step forth and let your day begin, and don't be surprised at the way that Love comes before you and brings you new ways to celebrate this wholeness and to remember that I Am your supply and that your heart is the conduit for your world.

Thus what you are guided to do will be supported from the highest resonance and what you feel will be the communion of Love on every level, in every area of your life, until every breath is a celebration and acknowledgement and every moment is a prayer of gratitude when the New World shows up unimpeded and you live every moment through your heart.

From Jesus

How Man Receives The Divine Love

(from askrealJesus.com)

I am here, Jesus;

I desire to write you a message on the question of: *'How the soul of a mortal receives the divine love and what its effect is, even though subsequently his mind may indulge in those beliefs that may tend to prevent the growth of the soul.'*

As you know, the inflowing of this love is caused by its bestowal by the Holy Spirit in response to sincere prayer and longings. I mean prayer and longings for the love itself, and not prayers in general for the material benefits that men more often and more naturally ask for and desire. The prayers of mortals for these things that may tend to make them successful and happy in their natural love are answered also if it be best that they should be, but these are not the prayers that bring the divine love or cause the Holy Spirit to work with men.

As the prayers of the sincere, earnest soul ascend to the Father, that soul becomes opened up to the inflowing of this love, and the soul's perceptions enlarge and come more in rapport with the conditions or influence that always accompanies the presence of this love, and consequently its entrance into the soul becomes easier and its reception more perceptible to the soul sense. The more earnest the prayer and sincere the longings, the sooner faith comes and with this faith, the realization that the divine love is permeating the soul.

When once the divine love finds a lodgment in the soul, it, to the extent that it receives the love, becomes as it were, a changed substance, partaking of the essence of the love. And as water may become colored by an ingredient foreign to itself and which changes not only its appearance but its qualities, so this divine love changes the appearance and qualities of the soul, and this change of qualities continues ever thereafter. The natural qualities of the soul and the essence of the love become One and united, and the soul is made altogether different in its constituency from what it was before the inflowing of the love, but this only to the extent of the love received.

As this love increases in quantity, the change and transformation becomes correspondingly greater until at last the transformation may and will become so great that the whole soul becomes a thing of this divine essence and partakes of its very nature and substance, a being of Divinity.

When once this love enters and truly possesses the soul and works the change mentioned, it, the love, never leaves nor disassociates itself from the soul. Its character of divine essence never changes to that of the mere natural love, and so far as it is present sin and error have no existence because it is just as impossible for this essence and sin and error to occupy the same parts of the soul at the same time as it is for two material objects to occupy the same space at the same time, as your philosophers say.

Divinity never gives place to that which is not of the divine. Man is working towards the attainment of the divine when he pursues the way provided for obtaining the divine nature. And as he advances and obtains a portion of this Divinity, no matter how small, he can never retrace his steps to the extent of ridding himself of this transforming essence and again become without its presence.

But this does not mean that a man may not lose the consciousness of the existence of this essence within his soul, for he frequently does. The indulgence of his carnal appetites and evil desires will place him in the condition that he may cease to have a consciousness of the existence of the divine love in his soul, and to himself he will be as if he had never had any experience of the change that I speak of.

And while this love can never be eradicated by the evils that man may indulge in or by the mental beliefs that he may acquire, yet the progress of this love in his soul may be checked and become stagnant as if the love were not, and sin and error may appear to be the only dominant elements of his life and being. But yet when once possessed, the love cannot be crowded out of his soul by sin and error, no matter how deep and intense they may be. I know that this may seem strange and impossible to man's intellectual thinking, and that it is not in accordance with what has been attributed to me as teaching that a soul may be lost. Nevertheless, a soul that has once received this divine essence cannot be lost, though its want of realization of the presence of this love and its awakening from its dormant condition caused by sin and error and its misdirected beliefs may delay its manifestation of life and existence for a long time, and much suffering and darkness may have to be endured by the soul that is in such a condition.

And it must not be understood by this as meaning that a soul cannot be lost, for it can, and many have been and will be. And many will realize the fact when too late.

Now, what is a lost soul? Not one that a man may actually lose in the sense of being deprived of it - separated from it actually, or even as regards his consciousness of not having a soul - for while at times he may believe that he has lost his soul in the sense of not having any, yet he is mistaken, for the soul, which is the man, can never be separated from himself, and as long as he lives in the physical body or in the spiritual body his soul will be with him.

And yet he may have a soul, consciously or not, and at the same time have lost it. This may seem a paradox to the mortal intellect or to the intellect of spirit, but it is true.

Then what is a lost soul? When God gave to man a soul, that soul was made in the image but not the substance of its Maker, and at the same time there was bestowed on him the privilege of having that soul become of the substance of the Father and to an extent divine and entitled to and capable of living in the celestial kingdom of the Father where everything is of the divine essence and nature. When the first parents by their act of disobedience forfeited that privilege, their souls lost the possibility of being of the divine nature and at-One with the Father in His kingdom, and they thereby lost not the natural soul, which was a part of their creation, but the soul having the possibility of obtaining the essence of Divinity and immortality as the Father has immortality.

As I have said heretofore, with my coming this great privilege was restored to mankind and the lost soul became again the object of man's recovery. And now he has that privilege as did the first parents before the fall, but also men may lose it as did they. As with the first parents, their souls were lost until they received into it the divine essence of the Father, so with men now, their souls are lost until and unless they receive this divine essence therein. As the first parents by their disobedience and refusal forfeited their privilege of having their souls become a living, divine substance, so now men by their disobedience and refusal will forfeit their privilege to save their souls from separation from the divine unity with the Father.

The lost soul is as real as the verities of the Father's immutable laws, and only by the operation of the divine love can the soul lost become the soul found.

Men may believe and teach that within them is a part of the divine that will cause their souls to progress and develop until it reaches the condition of Divinity that will make it a part of the Divinity of the Father, but in this they are all wrong, for while man was the highest creation of God, and the most perfect and made in His image, yet in man is no part of the divine, and having no part of the divine it is wholly impossible for him to progress to the possession of the divine. He, of himself, no matter what his development may be, can never become greater or more perfect or of a higher nature than he was at his creation.

The divine comes from above, and when once planted in a man's soul there can be no limit to its expansion and development, even in the celestial heavens. Let all men seek this love and there will be no lost souls not having the divine essence of the Father.

Your brother and friend, Jesus

It is Your Nature to Roam the Divine Cosmos Freely
(By JesusthroughJohn.com)

Within the illusion time expands and contracts, it is unreal and unreliable, and yet as you experience it it appears to move in a regular and linear fashion from the past, with all its memories, momentarily and continuously through the present, and into the uncertainty of a future that you try to forecast and pin down . . . and then something quite unexpected occurs! And that is one extremely good reason for living in the now! If you make a point of living in this now moment and dealing with events, situations, issues, and problems as they occur, relying on your intuition – the wisdom of your real Self – all will flow far more smoothly for you.

Trying to second guess what may happen tomorrow, next week, or next year intensifies the levels of stress that you experience through living in the darkness of the illusion – darkness because the Light of God's Love is hidden from you by the cloak or fog of the illusion. To see clearly, you have to leave the illusion and all its concepts and logic far behind you. All the inspiring insights that the great minds among you have discovered over the eons have have been revealed to them when they were not anchored by the limits that the illusion imposes upon you, but when they were as it were roaming free through the cosmos of their unlimited minds, ignoring all the preconceptions and cultural beliefs that may have suggested that what they were seeking was an impossible dream, unreal, a myth.

It is your nature to roam the divine cosmos freely, unfettered by logical human thought that invents rules based on inadequate understanding which then severely limits your creative abilities. Rules restrain and limit you unnaturally. They are, however, very convenient aspects of the illusion where separation seems substantial, and tangible, and they provide a framework that ensures, for instance, that people driving motor vehicles do not, on the whole, collide with each other because they are all following the same rules in a rather crowded environment. That aspect of rules is very useful as you struggle with the stresses and anxieties of daily living because it provides guidelines that enable you to be reasonably certain that your personal safety is assured.

What has happened over the eons is that many of the rules and regulations have become an inflexible and unquestioned overlay to all that you do, rather like an open prison, severely restricting your creative abilities in the form of imaginary blockages to progress – it is a bit like being in a room with many doors or exits, all but one of which are wide open, and you can only see the one that is closed and think that you are therefore unable to leave. In the last few decades there has been enormous growth in the numbers questioning all the rules, and this is very healthy.

God created you FREE! You chose to restrict yourselves by building the illusion and enclosing yourselves within it, and finally you are questioning it on a massive scale and coming to a collective realization that it is an asylum for the insane!

It was insane to build the illusion. It was a totally unrealistic and impossible attempt to separate yourselves from God because He is All that exists, and therefore separation from Him is impossible. He created you in Love and gave you everything that He had – infinite Love, infinite Wisdom, infinite Knowledge, infinite Power, and endless creative abilities and opportunities – and you chose to leave them all behind and enclose yourselves in a state of unreality where you eschewed those gifts to engage in the competitive destruction of one another, endlessly throughout the eons.

It matters not what you achieve through your constant and determined human efforts – wealth, position, recognition, power – because all of these are ephemeral, they do not and cannot last, and the very limited satisfaction that they provide fades rapidly. Your true home is with God, you know that, and nothing else can ever satisfy your intense need to be one once more with Him.

It has taken a long time for you to come to that realization and make the collective choice and decision to engage once again with Love so that the illusion can dissolve back into the nothingness from which you imagined it into existence. Every moment you spend within, in your quiet inner sanctuary, intending to be loving, compassionate, and accepting, accelerates the rate at which the illusion is crumbling.

All the spiritual channels, all those in the spiritual realms keep stressing the vital importance of attending to your personal spiritual practices daily because that is how you awaken. It expresses an overriding intent to awaken, to know and experience the Reality and the Oneness that is your real and eternal nature. It is what everyone who ever engaged with the illusion has sought and is seeking. Deep within every sentient being is the knowing that you are One with God, the Source from which all that exists flows in endless Love. By choosing to give credence to the illusion you have hidden that knowing from yourselves, and it is that apparent loss that is so painful for you. Nothing can be satisfactorily substituted for that all-encompassing sense of acceptance that Oneness and the Love that is Its nature provides, nothing!

And there is only Oneness, there is no beyond or outside, no past or future, there is just now at One with

Source. When you awaken, as you will, the joy and wonder that replaces all your doubts, anxieties, and fears will enfold you in a state of unimaginable ecstatic bliss. Go within daily, hourly if you can, and bring it to fruition, because that is what you are here to do.

Your loving brother, Jesus

The Truth Concerning Disease

I am here, Jesus

It is true that God never created anything of evil or that which is not in harmony with His nature and essence, which are only good, and that to ascribe the existence of evils and discords to God is erroneous and blasphemous. But the fact remains that these things exist and the mere denial of their existence does not remedy the harmful results that flow from such existence.

Man suffers from evil and error and disease, and has always so suffered since the fall from his state of perfection, and always will suffer in consequence of their being in his consciousness these things of reality. First arises the necessity of understanding how and by what means these things came into existence, and then it will become easier for the understanding of the means and the way by which they may be eliminated from the life and apparent nature of mankind.

As I have already told you, these things foreign to God's creation, were created by man alone in following out the suggestions and desires of his animal appetites. Then man must understand that these excrescences (abnormal impurities) to his perfect creation are real and existing, and result in his own damnation and alienation from the good, and are antagonistic to his original and natural condition of perfection, and 'that' they cannot be swept out of existence by the mere assertion that they are not real. The will, however, is the great force that must be used in the destruction of these excrescences, and as this will power in men is free and untrammeled, and in its operations follows the suggestions and desires of the appetites, both animal and spiritual, of man, it therefore becomes apparent that these appetites and desires must first be controlled and directed in that direction that will cause the will to be exercised in such a manner as to lead the thoughts and deeds towards the realization of the desires and appetites in harmony with God 's laws. Of course, in this effort he will have to use his mind and his emotional and affectionate nature, which are not of the mind but of the soul. As man is a creator as well as a creature, and as these things are the creatures of man alone, then, so far as the being of man is involved, they have a reality which will persist until their creator, man, has destroyed them.

Your brother and friend, Jesus

Maximal Healing

Not only does each one of you has a guide, one who is totally Awake, standing at your service, you also have me standing with you at your service. And then in addition to your guide there are those Awakened Individualities who working in conjunction with your guide on your behalf, relative to your physical well-being. They do not manipulate the body, but they stand helping to uncover whatever beliefs are blocking the normal function of your body and facilitating their release. And so what I encourage you to do every night when you go to bed, is to just say, "Will my healing team please address this _____ problem. I would like a healing session, and I would like it to be maximal". Not that the support that is given is less than maximal, but by saying "and let it be maximal", it is a matter of your giving permission consciously for the healing to be maximal.

Now in addition to this, when you eat, and before you put a bite of anything into your mouth I want you to bless it. I want you to thank God for this bite to eat. I want you to thank it for whatever its Real Meaning is. And I want you to remember that I am telling you that because God is indivisible. God cannot be conflicted. And therefore, the Kingdom of Heaven which is the only thing you are experiencing at this moment, even if you believe otherwise, because this is the Kingdom of Heaven, there is nothing in it that can have a conflicted effect. And therefore, this food that you are about to be putting in your mouth and swallowing has not the capacity, truly, divinely to conflict in any way with your body.

So I want you to express gratitude for the bite of food that's on the fork. I want you to thank God for it. And I want you to remember, consciously, that it has not the capacity to act at odds with you in anyway. Because if it exists at all and if your body exists at all it exists as the unconflicted presence or manifestation of an undivided God.

The more you can dare to look at your world, even as specifically as the bite of food on your plate, with the curiosity to experience what of God is expressed here, that is the way you can get past medical definitions of it, scientific definitions of it, and false beliefs that you have acquired about what it must be. And in that way, begin to experience the harmony that all of this is expressing.

Now I don't care how many years this has been going on. Twenty years of darkness has not built up a strength of presence that would hold back the light when the light went on. And six years of the presence of some condition does not acquire substance and therefore some permanence of presence that will be difficult to dissolve in the presence of clarity of mind and conscious expressions of appreciation which are forms of love.

So it doesn't have to take a year to get over this. It doesn't have to take three weeks. What I am saying is: do not say, "well, this has been going on for so long that it really is going to take awhile to go away." When the light of truth goes on, that which had no substance....true substance....must end up not being anywhere to be found.

Your body is your friend. Your body has a function. And that is to identify the presence of your Individuality perfectly. And your Individuality is the presence of God. So at the bottom line, the function of your body is to identify the presence and movement and meaning that God is, right there perfectly. It is used mainly to communicate love.

So don't hate your body, and don't try to rise above it and don't try to get beyond it. It must be brought right into the middle of the presence of God. It must be equated WITH God, not left on the outside. And then the same thing with anything you put in your mouth. And I do mean anything, including poison. That is an extreme, but I do not suggest that you try, because the clarity needed for that, because of the beliefs about it is great. However, my point is that there is no substance that you can find anywhere that can act in conflict with your body, because either it's all God perceived clearly or through a glass darkly. There is no other choice, you see!

You see, your body has no capacity to act independently because its whole function is to identify the presence of your Individuality perfectly. It's incapable of doing anything else. Nevertheless, all of you can, by means of fear and worry, you can seem to bias the function. You can't truly, totally override it, but you can bias your experience of it so that you experience distress. And what we're talking about is getting rid of this tendency to bias, so that the divine intent can re-emerge because you're not interfering with it anymore. So it's important for you to understand that your body is your ally because it has only one purpose....to identify you perfectly.

If you will get out of the way and let it do that, you will find it returning to its normal function. In other cases, you will find healing occurring....shortened limbs becoming extended, blemishes disappearing, enlarged breast for small busted women.... (someone giggles) Did I get you? So that symmetry and balance and the beauty that's inherent in the Movement of Love that God Is, is embodied.

So there's great benefit in having a new sense of what the body is and what its function is, and who this you is that it is identifying perfectly. Because it's not just a puny little human being that it's identifying perfectly, it's the presence of what God is being right there that it is identifying perfectly.

So you are embracing a new concept of body and a clearer idea of what you Are. And when your thought is in alignment with truth, with what is Really going on, as I said before, it will seem to you that the Universe conspires to conform to that evidence, or that manifestation. It isn't that you I have exercised power, but by getting your beliefs out of the way there is nothing distorting your experience of what's Really going on.

Cut out or print this (below) and place it at your bedside and use it to ask the Holy Spirit, your guides, and Jesus for help with an illness or disease at each and every bedtime, until all symptoms have left. Don't waver, be persistent and dedicated to your wellness that God has promised you.

I would like a healing session, and I would like it to be maximal.

Will my healing team please address this problem?:_____

_____

I am willing to let go of my beliefs that are blocking this healing. Thank you for your continued guidance and support. I love you all.

Print this below, and place in a conspicuous spot where you eat. Use it before you take the first bite, every time you sit down to eat, until it becomes natural and important to always bless your food in this way.

Thank you God for this food and this body, which both are an extension and expression of your love and bounty. Because this food is imbued with your love, I bless it, knowing that it cannot harm me in any way. I let go of any beliefs that are opposed to this truth. Likewise, I give the care of this body over to the Holy Spirit, my higher self.

(For healthy digestion, eat slowly and chew your food well)

Release Yourself from Fear by Embracing Love

Waiting is difficult for you. Here in the spiritual realms, where time is not an issue, we do understand this aspect of the illusion as many of us have had lives as humans. In the spiritual realms all is always just as it should be, perfect. Within the illusion more and more of you are opening to the Tsunami of Love and to the awareness that you are, each and every one of you, on a spiritual path or, if you prefer, a spiritual mission to assist humanity to awaken and dispel the illusion.

To do that you have to be human! And that means that you are, to a certain extent--in fact to a very large extent indeed, unaware of the absolute brilliance with which the divine entity that each of you is, shines forth, constantly. You were created perfect and you remain perfect for all eternity. But to enter the illusion as humans to assist humans in the awakening process it was essential that you became like them, lost, confused, and seemingly abandoned in a fearfully threatening and unforgiving world. It *IS* unreal, but it seems wholly real, all that exists, to the vast majority of humans, and death seems like the end, the termination point of a brief, unsatisfying, and pointless life. An unfair and unreasonable experience that gives you no choices of your own that would allow you to alter it to suit your rightful needs and desires.

The illusion is your conception, your institution, your *dream or nightmare* depending on how you are experiencing and interpreting it. For eons it seemed that it was a given that you had to accept and cope with, but in the last hundred years modern psychology has begun to show you that you *can* change your experience by changing your mind about it. You can choose to feel overwhelmed by the situations that seemingly envelop you, and collapse under them remaining a crushed and helpless victim of circumstances, or you can choose to accept life as it is presented to you, deal with the situations with which it apparently confronts you, and move forwards.

Life is *always* about this *now* moment. However, you have managed to lose sight of that, and you focus massively on the past in vain attempts to prevent it from recurring in the future, or to ensure that it does recur in the future. But, there is *only* the now moment, and everything that affects you, that influences you in any way happens in this now moment. The other problem for you is that the now moment seems so brief. Could such a brief, ill-considered thought, word, or momentary motion or activity truly cause such an enormously unexpected outcome? The answer is a resounding yes!

You do create your own reality by the thoughts, words, and actions with which you engage. Your problem, as humans, is that in the restricted environment that you appear to inhabit it is very difficult to foresee the possible consequences to which they lead. You collectively chose to build an environment that was severely restrictive, limiting, and uncertain, because you wanted to experience that uncertainty and the confusion that it produced. And now, after eons of pain and suffering, you have collectively decided that enough is enough.

Having made that very sensible decision you have then needed to ascertain the way forwards out of your endless suffering and into a state of lasting peace. "How is peace possible?" you ask one another as you observe the vast number of conflicts, distrusts, and betrayals that you observe all across the world? Peace is impossible you declare, because of all those unstable and violent ones who would maintain a constant state of war because it gives them power, control, and wealth. And so you conclude that armies and weapons are an essential form of defense against those misguided, one must sin in order to maintain peace. That is an insane belief, as you know in your hearts, but fear prevents you from acknowledging that one truth that would set you free.

As all the channels are repeatedly telling you "LOVE is the ONLY answer to all the problems that you experience." Yes, if you embrace love, it seems to you that you are laying yourselves open to permanent abuse, pain, and suffering by making yourselves insanely vulnerable. But, on the other hand, you *know* deep within yourselves that Love is THE answer. What the spiritual channels are doing, and what you Light workers, starseeds, and wayshowers are doing is fearlessly embracing the Love field that eternally supports you, and demonstrating by your faith, and by the results that occur in your immediate lives, that this is true.

AND where people are refusing the Love, and refusing to trust, the conflicts, suffering, and betrayals continue, endlessly. There are now more than enough of you on Earth actively demonstrating Love as a way of life, the only way of life, the Real way of life, to bring lasting peace to your confused and suffering multitudes. Keep on loving and watch your relationships – personal, societal, business, and international – stabilize, warm, develop, forgive, accept, and become as one. You know it makes sense, and that nothing else does.

Remember, you are *eternally and infinitely* supported by your loving Father, and therefore by all sentient life forms that our Father has created. The only opposition is from a few, a very few, a tiny minority of insane ego-driven souls in human form who can only achieve their aims *if* you support them. Just stop supporting them. Your only reason for doing so is because you are fearful, believing that you are small, insignificant beings in a vast and threatening universe, and you *fall* for the egoic blusterings of these few insane and utterly misguided ones who would persuade you that Love is weak and that you need their strength – but they have no strength! And to fall for that line of reasoning is also insane.

You are all divine beings created from Love by God for eternal joy. That state is available to you right *now! Wake up and embrace your Father, the divine field of Love, the Tsunami of Love that surrounds and supports you in every moment!* Release yourselves from fear by embracing Love, and watch with amazement as those few misguided ones who would control you fade away into the unreality of the dissolving illusion.

Your loving brother, Jesus.

3. Help from Other Writers

From Matt Kahn
Transformation Manifesto

We live in a unique point in history-a precipice of human transformation. WE ARE AWAKENING... We are no longer content with living someone else's dream. We long for something more. We are on a mission to change the world. We don't have a message, we have a MOVEMENT.

We've unplugged from the matrix. We don't just make a change, we totally transform. It's not that we have no fear, it's that we do it anyway. THE STATUS QUO MAKES US GAG. It's a life worth living or nothing at all. We are not going to settle. We don't wait for a catastrophe to change: we consciously evolve. We value integrity. We question authority. We rewrite our scripts, we release limitations, we let go of that which does not serve us and when we're not motivated, WE DREAM BIGGER. We TAKE RESPONSIBILITY for our lives and we TAKE ACTION! We turn curses into blessings. We use our gifts and share them with the world. We are grateful. We enjoy the simple things in life. We breathe. We live. We dance in the rain. We know that happiness is a CHOICE and WE CHOOSE TO LIVE an audacious life. We are authentically, totally, and emphatically US. We own it. We don't apologize. We ARE Transformation.

From Joel Goldsmith
Prayer For Healing

Be not captive of yourself and your mind, but be set free as you were designed to be.

I command complete healing within the attitudes, thought patterns, beliefs, and memories of the mind by the power and authority of the Holy Spirit, my authentic Self.

I bind spirits of depression, confusion, discouragement, fear, and anger and cast them out and away, never to return.

The glory of God now floods my mind, spirit, and soul and drives out all negative thoughts and ideas that create suffering and disease.

God's grace is now raining down upon me, completely soaking me in His love, transforming and renewing me into complete deliverance.

God's word declares it for me.

God's will authorizes it and His Holy Spirit delivers it.

It is done and finished in the name of Jesus Christ.

How to Make Yourself Unhappy, Miserable, and Lonely
(just in case you've run out of ideas)

Make yourself sick, with negative thoughts.

Create chaotic conditions in your life.

Focus your attentions on your errors and "their" errors.

Be arrogant and righteous.

Feel guilty and offer guilt to others.

Become very busy at non-essentials.

Whatever you give..........look to get something back.

Do a lot of comparing and analyzing.

Be possessive and stingy.

Be poor and be a victim.

Have a strong need to equalize.

See rejection everywhere.

Blame yourself or others for everything.

Constantly link the past to the future.

See unfairness whenever possible.

Concentrate on your "failures" and those of others.

Contradict yourself, and others whenever possible.

Procrastinate and delay whenever possible.

Have a strong sense of competition.

Dwell on a sense of danger at every opportunity.

Separate yourself often from others and your spiritual tools.

Make everything complex.

Concentrate on retaliation and loss.

Believe all your thoughts.

And of course, be sure to keep a list of errors and itemize them often.

4. Freedom Worksheets

Love Yourself More (worksheet)

As human beings, we have many needs that are important to us, which is perfectly normal. Needs are natural and when they are met in a healthy and balanced way, we are most happy. The problem comes up when we look to others to get those needs met instead of giving them to God. We are often unconscious of our most indispensable needs! But other people can usually spot them a mile away, and instead of giving us what we want, they are inclined to do the opposite! Such is the nature of needs. They scare people away instead of drawing them to us. Emotionally needy people are not much fun to be around---they will manipulate, dominate, and use finesse in an attempt to get what they want. And when others turn away, they may get annoyed, angry, or blaming.

You may have experienced this a time or two yourself. However, this frustrating cycle can go on for a lifetime until one makes a conscious decision to change. When you become less needy and take responsibility for your own needs, you become free. You are more open and receptive, more loving and much more attractive to other people.

The first step is to identify what your needs are. Once you have done this inner work, you will notice that people respond to you much more to your liking. Being totally honest with yourself, check off your needs below.

I need to feel:

Loved

Cherished

Admired

Smart

Authoritative

Creative

Important

Valued

Beautiful

Successful

Adored

Respected

Confident

In control

Seen

Connected

Unique

Validated

Recognized

Desirable

Secure

Prosperous

Healthy

Wealthy

Appreciated

Add your own below:

Now circle your three top needs, and honestly list how you typically attempt to get them met through others.
#1 need:
How I meet this need:

#2 need:
How I meet this need:

#3 need:
How I meet this need:

How much time do you wait for others to provide you with you what you need? How often does that approach really work....very rarely, right? The better approach is to love yourself more. When you love yourself, your emotional energy vibrates "cleaner" and at a higher frequency.
What follows are 8 ways to love yourself more:
1). Accept your whole self. Accept your greatness and your limitations. You are a vital and vibrant human being, start feeling good about yourself just the way you are right now!
2). Believe in yourself. Be confident in yourself and your talents/abilities. Have faith that the universe will provide and that your needs will ultimately be met for the highest good.

3). Consider yourself. Reflect about your likes, dislikes, what you want and don't want. You deserve to have the best relationships, career, and lifestyle.

4). Discover yourself. Learn about your personality, values, and beliefs through assessment tools and inspirational books. Excavate your soul and create your life around what is most precious to you.

5). Encourage yourself. You are worthy of special treatment! Say and do nice things for yourself every day. Keep a running accomplishment list and add to it regularly.

6). Expand yourself. Explore the world around you. Get interested in what life has to offer. Read books, meet people, take classes, or travel to new countries. Get in the habit of doing things differently.

7). Forgive yourself. Let go of any residual guilt or fear from your past. Forgive yourself for making mistakes and not getting everything "exactly right." When you forgive, you free up emotional energy that can better used to love and be loved.

8). Value yourself. Just by being born, you are worthy of esteem and value. Let yourself off the hook and move away from having to do anything to deserve to be valued. Treat yourself like you would a best friend. You deserve to get all of your needs met, and you are really the only one capable of filling that need. Know that YOU are the MOST important person in your life. You will always be in relationship with yourself, so make it the best relationship it can be. When you love and value yourself and tend to your own needs, the result is your cup overflows, with more to be shared. This becomes very attractive to others.

Free copies of this worksheet are available by emailing Jonathan... jmathews6565@gmail.com. This material may be copied and shared.

Mastery of Life Worksheet

There is work to be undertaken that will guarantee your freedom and spiritual success. First mark each area you feel you have already mastered, then afterward summarize in a paragraph your intent (commitment) for the next area you choose to work on, and allow a realistic period of time to be complete with it. Just complete one at a time and don't set yourself up to fail! Master all these areas of your life and your freedom, peace, joy, and wellbeing will be assured. People will hardly even recognize you! You will have mastered life!

- (mastered___) I give up not feeling worthy. I am perfect, whole, and complete, just as God created me. My past mistakes and thoughts have no impact on the truth of who I am. I am God incarnate. I am extraordinary, a unique expression of God's love. I am the beneficiary of God's wisdom and abundance. I am good and innocent.

- (mastered___) I make no decisions by myself; I first call on the Holy Spirit, my true Self, for guidance. I surrender my will to His, knowing that His will IS my will. Then all my decisions will be based in love and they will benefit myself and all others concerned. I will learn that the Holy Spirit always is and always has been my friend and confidant.

- (mastered___) I see another's interest as my own and I see his suffering as my own. If I see there is a need, it is MINE to fill. I ask for guidance from the Holy Spirit, my true Self, as to how I can be truly helpful. Because we are one, when I give to my brother/sister, I give to myself. My greatest assets become my patience, love, and kindness. With some practice, this process will become natural without really thinking about it. As a side effect, your heart will be constantly filled with love and joy.

- (mastered___) I do not judge because I'm unable to. I can choose again. I can love everyone just the way they are, without needing to change anything or anyone. (I cannot be against anything unless I have first judged it.) It will be enlightening to notice how often your mind is consumed with judgment in the course of a day. Without judgment, you will become so much more peaceful, joyful, and content.

- (mastered___) When I am seemingly attacked, I ask the Holy Spirit to help me see it differently. Instead of being defensive, I ask myself how I can best serve this seeming perpetrator, knowing that he/she is hurting and needs love. I let go of pride, anger, and condemnation so that I can experience peace and joy, which are my birthright!

- (mastered___) I stay in integrity. My thoughts, words, and deeds are unconflicted. I always speak the truth, as I know it. This allows me self respect, self esteem, and self love. In other words, I can always trust myself.

- (mastered___) I give over all my fears to the Holy Spirit. I am not a body, I am free. There is nothing to fear. I surrender the fear of death, suffering, lack, and loss. There is no greater illusion than fear. I can trust God instead.

- (mastered___) I provide selfless service whenever appropriate. I give of my time, talents, and money. I do not ask for or expect anything in return, not even recognition. I practice giving anonymously. I give knowing that I simultaneously give to myself. I cannot out give God.

- (mastered___) I listen carefully to the criticisms and advice of others and ask the Holy Spirit for the truth that can assist me on my spiritual path. I don't condemn the person or make him/her wrong, even in my mind, but instead see him as a potential gift. I keep an open mind and heart; I would rather be happy than be right or righteous.

- (mastered___) I pay attention to my thoughts, words, and beliefs, for they create my reality. I assume full responsibility (not blame) for what I have created, knowing that I can always choose DIFFERENT words, beliefs and thoughts. I think only about what I like and want, not what I don't want, so that I can manifest appropriately. I let go of beliefs that no longer serve me. I take action when needed to assist me in creating more appropriate manifestations.

- (mastered___) I give up my stories that keep me imprisoned in the past. I can instead live in the now, where God is. I accept God's grace instead of suffering. Without my stories I can move effortlessly through life. I no longer think my stories are who I am and they don't control my destiny!

- (mastered___) I replace illusions (the world) for love (God). I give up chasing people, pleasure, power, and things. I surrender any need for respect, approval, and support. I choose instead to focus on the joy of who I am. I let go of anything that would cause me stress. (See section or paper on stress)

- (mastered___) I let go of control, attachments, and outcomes. This is big! I can choose WHAT IS instead.

I give up thinking that I can change circumstances or change another so that I can be happy. They have nothing to do with my peace and happiness, which is only in my mind. I can leave my body be as it is, knowing that it is perfect for my path through life. I accept its size, shape, and state of health. I am only happy because I am aware of, and extending, the love that I am. I give all outcomes to God.

- (mastered___) I can forgive both myself and everyone; I can know and see our true innocence. I forgive my beliefs and projections of my illusions and wrong thinking. There are actually no perpetrators and no victims. In truth, there is only love. I can see attacks for what they are, a call for love and nothing more and I will respond, WITH love and nothing else.

- (mastered___) I am in a constant state of gratitude because it feels good while it is undoing the ego. I cannot be in gratitude and simultaneously suffer. When conflicted with a brother, I can use appreciation and acceptance to replace judgment. I find more and more to be thankful for. I am grateful even when circumstances are difficult because I can never see the whole picture. I trust God impeccably to provide the lessons I need for my healing.

- (mastered___) I give up duality. There is only good and that is God, who is in everything and everyone.

Anything else in my mind that is not love is not real or true. I have put my own meaning on everything; otherwise it is neutral, not good or bad. The good news is, I can live IN this world of duality, but not be OF it.

- (mastered___) I let go of the world's views concerning security. I truly know that there is no security in this world! No kind of money, insurance, medicine, doctors, or any other kind of protection is of value to me. I am not attached to keeping this body alive. I only trust and rely on God, my source. I am free.

- (mastered___) I can die to the ego. This is what it means to be born again. I can let go of the ego that thinks it needs something and instead rely on the Holy Spirit, that part of me that is complete, wise, and loving. I am not the ego, I am free and I open my mind to all possibilities. I humbly accept my ego's nothingness, allowing my real Self to shine through.

- (mastered___) I am devoted to doing my spiritual work regularly. That may include prayer, meditation, and spiritual literature. My life is a prayer and God is always in my mind. I am not a body, I am Spirit, therefore I am free, just as God intended!

I give you this guide with heartfelt love, knowing that with it's regular use, your suffering will be alleviated and your life will transform.

Free copies of this worksheet are available by emailing Jonathan… jmathews6565@gmail.com. This material may be copied and shared.

Healing my Emotional Wounds of the Past
My Upset Worksheet dated _____.

In order to receive maximal benefit from this healing worksheet, please take your time and thoroughly contemplate each question and suggestion.

1.Choose either A or B below:

A. I think I am upset because(person)_____
did /didn't /said (circle one)_____
_____

B. I think I am upset because of the following event:_____
_____

The truth is: My upset is strictly internal, unique to me, and is created out of my own thoughts and beliefs from the past!

2. My feelings concerning this upset: (see negative emotions below)
_____

3. My punishment and retaliatory thoughts toward others:_____
_____
_____

Toward myself:_____
_____
_____

4. Where in my past did I learn this defensive posturing, or by whom?_____
_____

The truth is: I punish and blame only when my denied and repressed emotions are triggered, and has little to do with what anyone said or did, or what happened.

5. In order to avoid this truth and the resulting guilt and pain, I have: (Circle ones that apply)

A. Gotten angry, blamed the other, stewed and mentalized about how wrong they are, and what nerve they have.

B. Eaten, smoked, drank, drugged, or worked obsessively.

C. Found others that would agree with me.

D. Other:_____

6. Other thoughts I think and the beliefs I believe, that are related to this upset:_____

_____

_____

_____

7. Because this upset is causing me pain and suffering, I choose to get to the bottom line truth of this scenario. I ask for assistance from (circle one or more): God, Holy Spirit, my guide, my facilitator, Jesus

The truth is: I am not upset for the reason I think, I have merely triggered a buried and denied emotion, a thought or belief in my subconscious from the past that I need to heal. If I am in pain, I am the one who has healing to do.

8. What is my recurring story, my repeating pattern, directly related to this upset? _____

_____

_____

9. How does this story or pattern relate to an earlier emotional incident in my life possibly involving a caregiver or sibling? It could have also been done by myself, or I was accused of it._____

_____

_____

10.What do I really want? (peace, relief, forgiveness, happiness, serenity, closure)

_____

To have this, I am willing to look at this scenario differently and even go through the emotional, and possible physical symptoms of healing. I release my demands that other people or situations need to change, and I take full responsibility for my creations. I release my punishing thoughts, my judgements, my anger, resentments, guilt, and blame. I let go of old wounds, ideas, and beliefs that have been stored in my subconscious mind. I especially release my need to be right. I would rather be happy than right. If need be, I will do a worksheet whenever upset so that I may again discover the truth that will set me free.

11. After this forgiveness process, I feel: (see positive emotions below)_____

_____

I now see and understand
that:_____

_____

12. I am grateful for this upset, for it has shown me a new way to look at upsets. It has given me an opportunity to live my life in the here and now, with integrity and authenticity, leading to a more peaceful, joyous, and loving life. I now connect with love, my original and true nature.

Notes:

_____

_____

_____

_____

List of All Emotions (feelings)
Words Expressing Anger:
annoyed aggravated appalled disgusted dismayed bitter horrified nauseated cranky riled enraged exasperated frustrated furious hostile incensed infuriated irritated outraged provoked offended repulsed revolted ticked-off wary resentful steamed troubled upset vicious hateful angry hostile jealous
Words Expressing Hurt:
abused awful betrayed devalued terrible crippled distant diminished deflated forgotten put down deprived deserted dreadful intimidated oppressed damaged rotten insulted neglected slighted ignored isolated jilted defeated snubbed cheated persecuted offended rejected
Words Expressing Inadequacy: helpless incapable incompetent inadequate inept inferior powerless useless unworthy mediocre insignificant stupid
Words Expressing Embarrassment:
 foolish awkward mortified clumsy insecure silly ashamed conspicuous disgraced uncomfortable humiliated
Words Expressing Confusion:

baffled bewildered confused rattled distracted
dumbfounded flabbergasted flustered jarred jolted
muddled perplexed puzzled rattled anxious disconnected
dazed frustrated

Words Expressing Sadness:
anguished blue burdened dejected depressed down lost
despondent disappointed discouraged disheartened
downcast heavy-hearted gloomy let-down low melancholy
abandoned alone deserted empty excluded lonely
friendless ignored isolated jilted scorned rejected pathetic
slighted miserable moody pained troubled weary

Words Expressing Fear:
afraid boxed-in cornered fearful frightened jittery jumpy
nervous panicky scared shaken spooked terrified skeptical
threatened agitated uneasy unnerved overwhelmed
alarmed worried helpless insecure anxious

Positive Emotions, Words Expressing Happiness:
amused blissful charmed cheerful contented delighted
ecstatic elated excited fabulous fortunate giddy glad
gratified high joyful jubilant marvelous pleased proud
soothed thrilled tickled turned-on wonderful peaceful
excited loving relaxed secure serene thankful confident
proud important successful worthwhile powerful energetic
important appreciated optimistic pensive playful stimulated

Free copies of this worksheet are available by emailing
Jonathan… jmathews6565@gmail.com. This material may
be copied and shared.

Recommended Websites and Books

WEBSITES:

askrealjesus.com

johnsmallman2.wordpress.com   (Jesus through John)

progressivechristianity.org

truedivinenature.com (Matt Kahn on utube.com)

RECOMMENDED READING:

"A Course in Miracles"
"The Way of Mastery"
"Of Monkeys and Dragons" Michele O'Donnell
"The Art of Spiritual Healing" Joel Goldsmith
"Collected Essays of Joel Goldsmith" DeVorss Publications
"Divine Love" Wayne Dyer
"Practicing The Power of Now" Eckhart Tolle
"The Untethered Soul" Michael Singer
"Living A Course in Miracles" Jon Mundy
"A Thousand Names for Joy" Byron Katie
"The End of Reincarnation" Gary Renard
"A Return to Love" Marianne Williamson
"The Twelve Gateways to Freedom" Dan Millman
"The Spontaneous Healing of Belief" Gregg Braden
"The Path of Mindfulness Meditation" Peter Strong
"A New Earth" Eckart Tolle

www.ingramcontent.com/pod-product-compliance
Lightning Source LLC
Chambersburg PA
CBHW072201280526
45788CB00002B/828